THE FUTURE OF RENTAL HOUSING

George Sternlieb
and
James W. Hughes

CENTER
FOR URBAN
POLICY   RESEARCH

Published in the United States of America
by the Center for Urban Policy Research
Building 4051—Kilmer Campus
New Brunswick, New Jersey 08903

Library of Congress Cataloging in Publication Data
Main entry under title:

Sternlieb, George.
    The future of rental housing.

    Bibliography: p.
    Includes index.
    1. Rental housing—United States.
2. Housing—United States. I. Hughes,
James W.   II. Title.
HD7288.85.U6S75   363.5'8   81-10077
ISBN 0-88285-073-3 (pbk.)   AACR2

Cover design by Francis G. Mullen

Contents

List of Exhibits

Introduction

The deterioration of classic income housing cost relationships, and the dismantling of the financing mechanisms that have been built up over a generation, have raised very real questions concerning America's future shelter capacities.

Within the debate on the future shape and constituents of housing, there are practically an infinite number of permutations—but certainly central among them is the place and function of multifamily rental housing. As an amenity for middle-class occupancy (i.e., nontenement, nonshared facilities), this is a construct barely a hundred-years old. It rose parallel with the development of an urban middle class, and has declined with their outmigration. Even in the suburbs, the rise in housing standards and inflationary pressures of our time has raised significant question as to its future utility. It is the purpose of this text to explore the question of housing needs and affordability in the 1980s in the context of evolving national events and priorities, and thus provide a definition of the future role of rental housing.

America's housing problem has resolved itself into two basic and diverse phenomena. On the one hand, there is the Pandora's Box of inflationary expectation epitomized by the rate of increment in housing values that has made homeownership the premier middle-class collectible. The level of trading in, and trading up, is seemingly independent of the need elements that classically have been linked to household life cycles. It is rather a demonstration of the demand for "more" housing investment.

On the other end of the spectrum are those Americans who cannot afford to board the housing train; whose incomes are too low, or whose competence in securing a down payment is too limited. And this is the sphere of the market to which rental housing has been increasingly relegated. To the bulk of this group, housing as an investment is much more a dream, or a desirable fantasy, rather than possessing any kind of immediate potential. Shelter is much more strikingly the key to their needs; and the provision of this shelter is ever more difficult within the inflationary facts of life.

From a political perspective, the dilemma of the renter, at least on the national level, is accentuated by their distinct minority status. As one reads through the hearings and debates on housing legislation in the Congress, it is strikingly evident that rental tenure is viewed as transitional to the ultimate goal of ownership. The only exceptions are those too poor to ever support such a condition.

Forecasting is at best an imperfect art; the authors are all too conscious of the limitations not only of the art form, but of their exercise of it. The issues at hand, however, require at the very least a sharpening of definition—and it is to this goal that the work presented here is dedicated.

Detailed Summary of Findings

Housing Demand: The Evolving Profile of Rental Housing Consumers

Throughout the 1970s, the profile of renter household types evolved considerably. In part, this was a concomitant of national demographic shifts, of marked growth in single person and non-modular households. But it was also the consequence of a process that we have labeled the "cream skimming" of the rental market: the withdrawal of the more affluent household types—particularly husband-wife tenants—into ownership status. With income showing wide variation in accordance with household configuration, the household formats dominating rental housing portend an ominous lag in rent paying capacity in the future. The maturation of the "post-shelter" society—housing as investment as well as shelter—has made homeownership virtually a mandatory strategy for coping in an inflationary milieu. Only the truly affluent (or those too poor to care) can afford to ignore the tax and investment benefits of ownership tenure.

1. A major determinant of housing demand is the evolution of both the number and composition of the nation's households. Between 1970 and 1979, the total number of households increased by almost 14 million, an increment comparable to that of the growth in total population (approximately 15-million people) for the corresponding time interval.

2. The gains accruing to individual household types varied significantly, however. Husband-wife configurations represented the slowest growing household type, one parent families and non-family households the fastest. America's population is rapidly partitioning itself into an increasing number of varied, once considered "atypical," household arrangements.

3. When changing household profiles are sectored by tenure, sharp differentials are evident between owner and renter occupied sectors. Over the 1970 to 1978 time period, the following trends were operative:

   a. Of the total gains in owner households (10.9 million), 5.7 million were husband-wife configurations.

   b. The second largest growth sector comprised one-person households (2.8 million). However, the rate of increase (59.1 percent) of the latter was more than triple that of husband-wife households (18.4 percent).

   c. While "other male head" and "female head" configurations experienced smaller absolute growth increments, their rates of increase (44.6 and 44.3 percent, respectively) were also far greater than that registered by husband-wife households.

4. The rental sector, over the 1970 to 1978 period, exhibited tendencies of a substantially different nature:

   a. While the total number of renter households increased by 3.3 million, a loss of 2.6 million husband-wife households was concurrently experienced (-20.2 percent).

   b. One-person households, in contrast, increased by 3.2 million, or 50.0 percent. The growth rates for "other male head" (75.1 percent) and "female head" (56.5 percent) configurations were even higher, but their absolute growth increments were somewhat smaller in magnitude.

5. As a result of these household shifts, rental housing has assumed a much more limited and much more sharply defined functional role within the United States than held true in earlier years. With the declining presence of husband-wife households, rental facilities have become increasingly focused on nonmodular households. The rental sector has lost market penetration in areas that have been viewed as its traditional heartland—pre- and post-child rearing stages of the family life cycle.

6. When black central city renter households are isolated, the preceding phenomena are even more accentuated. While the number of husband-wife formats declined by one in four (25 percent) in the rental sector, female headed households increased by 56.9 percent and one-person households by 55 percent. By 1978, female headed households evolved into the dominant (37.4 percent of total) sector of the black central city rental market. The following profiles illustrate the overall contours of the phenomena:

Household Configurations	Total U.S. Households		Total U.S. Renter Households		Central City Black Renter Households	
	1970	1978	1970	1978	1970	1978
TOTAL HOUSEHOLDS	100.0	100.0	100.0	100.0	100.0	100.0
2-or-More Person Households	82.4	77.8	72.9	64.4	74.7	68.1
Male Head, Wife Present	68.7	60.5	54.1	37.9	40.1	24.6
Other Male Head	3.8	5.0	4.9	7.4	5.5	6.1
Female Head	9.9	12.3	13.9	19.0	29.1	37.4
1-Person Households	17.6	22.2	27.1	35.6	25.2	31.9

7. Attendant to the changing profiles of renter/owner household configurations are sharp distinctions in fiscal capacities and income levels. Husband-wife configurations, particularly when the wife is in the paid labor force, is the most affluent household type; however, it is this precise market sector that is vacating rental housing. Female and male headed households without spouse, and one-person households, are characterized by much lower income resources; these are the household types that are increasingly dominating the rental market.

8. The following income ratios are illustrative of the income differentials that are developing:

Household Configuration	1973 Renter/ Owner Ratio	1978 Renter/ Owner Ratio	1973 Black Renter/ Total Renter Ratio	1978 Black Renter/ Total Renter Ratio
TOTAL HOUSEHOLDS	.63	.55	.88	.70
2-or-More Person Households	.68	.58	.76	.69
Male Head, Wife Present	.73	.69	.88	.90
Other Male Head	.69	.63	.69	.91
Female Head	.73	.57	.91	.85
1-Person Households	1.13	1.09	.78	.77

By 1978, the income of all renter households was only 55 percent of owner income; concurrently, the income of black central city renters was only 70 percent of that of all renter households. The most competitive renter income household— male head, wife present—is rapidly withdrawing from rental tenure. This is particularly the case for black central city residents.

Future Demand: Owner Versus Rental

The precise share of the market that will be secured by the two tenurial forms (renter versus owner) clearly is subject to a vast complex of forces, not the least of them being the uncertain state of capital markets. Thus, any extrapolative projection proves to be a hazardous undertaking. Nonetheless, a "first approximation" forecast has been made, incorporating existing household projections of the Census Bureau (*Current Population Survey*), along with straight line projections of historic owner/renter shares as defined by historical *Annual Housing Survey* tabulations. The end result is an aggregate rental housing demand in the 1980s closely replicating that evidenced in the 1970s—a growth slightly in excess of 4.0-million households seeking rental accommodations. The major growth surge appears to remain the province of ownership tenure.

1. Recalibrating the *Annual Housing Survey* (AHS) and *Current Population Survey* (CPS) household typologies to a common format is necessary in order to project future demand for rental housing. A linear projection of historic owner/renter tenure shares (AHS) for each household configuration indicates the following trendlines to 1990:

	1970	1977	1980	1990
Male Head, Wife Present				
Owner	70.7	77.1	79.4	86.9
Renter	29.3	22.9	20.6	13.1
Male Head, Other				
Owner	41.2	38.6	37.6	33.9
Renter	58.8	61.4	62.4	66.1
Female Head, Other				
Owner	47.8	47.2	46.9	46.1
Renter	52.2	52.8	53.1	53.9

2. The CPS projection of future households by type reveals the following patterns:

	1970	1980	1990
TOTAL HOUSEHOLDS*	63,450	79,870	96,653
Husband-Wife	44,062	48,968	54,731
Male Head, Other	6,033	10,270	14,874
Female Head, Other	13,354	20,633	27,049

3. The product of both of the preceding projection sets is an estimation of future rental demand by household type (numbers in thousands):

Household Configuration*	1980	1990	Change: 1880 to 1990 Number	Percent
Total Renter	27,451	31,581	4,130	15.0
Male Head, Wife Present	20,087	7,170	- 2,917	- 28.9
Male Head, Other	6,408	9,832	3,424	53.4
Female Head, Other	10,956	14,579	3,623	33.1
Total Owner	52,420	65,073	12,653	24.1
Total Households	79,871	96,654	16,783	21.0

Thus, 4.1 million additional households will be seeking rental accommodations over the decade of the 1980s, despite a substantial shrinkage of "male head, wife present" households in the rental demand equation.

4. Concurrently, 12.6-million households are projected to require ownership tenure, resulting in an overall growth in households approaching 16.8 million.

5. This pattern of anticipated demand reflects the general maintenance of trends evidenced during the 1970s. Thus, the major gains that are indicated lie in the province of ownership demand:

	Change: 1970 to 1977	Average Annual Change
Renter Households*	2,954	422
Owner Households	8,800	1,269

	Change: 1980 to 1990	Average Annual Change
Renter Households	4,130	413
Owner Households	12,653	1,265

6. Thus, the projections are *not* indicative of abrupt discontinuities in long-term trendlines, but rather are representative of the mainstream of our experience in the past decade. While certainly not a certification of their accuracy, this consistency does suggest they represent a plausible "first approximation" scenario.

*Numbers in thousands.

Housing Supply: Changing Inventory Parameters

The rapid pace of household formation in the 1970s could only have proceeded in the context of a complementary expansion in the nation's supply. As the accounts of housing production over the decade are examined, it indeed becomes clear that record net inventory gains—both in terms of rental and owner housing—were achieved. It is difficult to avoid the impression, however, that whatever the scale of supply expansion, it was immediately matched by corresponding rates of household formation, i.e., population immediately diffuses into any inventory enlargement. The consumption, on a per-capita base, of increasing quantities of housing throughout the past decade has been unprecedented in the nation's housing annals. *Inexpensive housing supply begets households!*

1. From 1970 to 1978, over 15 million year-round housing units were added to the nation's housing inventory, an increment far greater than the 11-million net additions recorded over the *entire* 1960 to 1970 decade.

2. While the 1970 to 1978 gains of the renter occupied sector (3.3-million units) were but one-third of those registered by owner occupied units (10.4-million units), their absolute magnitude approached that of the entire preceding decade (3.3-million units). It is highly probable that the net rental gains of the 1970s will exceed that of any preceding intercensal decade, at least since 1920.

3. Thus, rental housing's declining share of the total inventory is not due to the lack of growth in this sector. It is the result of unparalleled expansion in homeownership during a decade that has been the most prolific housing period in America's history.

4. Indeed, the 1970s recorded an acceleration of long-term trends toward homeownership. As late as 1940, renter occupied units accounted for 56.4 percent of the total occupied housing stock. By 1978, the rental share declined to 34.8 percent. This long-term shift has been marked across all geographic partitions and racial groups.

5. The expansion of the rental sector has taken place principally in the suburban areas of SMSAs and in nonmetropolitan areas. By 1978, central cities accounted for only 43.9 percent of all renter occupied units. On a regional base, the South and West secured the largest shares of new construction, the Northeast

the smallest share. Within the latter region, only one out of ten (9.9 percent) renter occupied units was built from 1970 to 1978. In the South and West, the corresponding share was roughly one in five (22.1 and 20.0 percent, respectively).

6. As of 1978, the bulk of the nation's rental units (26.9-million total units) were located in 2- to 4-unit structures (7.4-million units) and one-family detached structures (7.2 million units). Only 2.5-million units were located in buildings containing 50 or more units. Thus, the supply of rental housing is far more heterogeneous than is sometimes understood.

7. At the same time, the actual scale of individual rental units is much more consistent than the structural configuration in which they are incorporated. The vast majority of rental units contain three to five rooms, with the median (4.0 rooms) remaining constant over the 1970 to 1978 period.

8. The 1970s also witnessed the increasing presence of full amenities in the rental inventory, at least as measured by complete kitchens, bathrooms, and full plumbing facilities.

9. Concurrently, however, the median monthly gross rent increased from $108 in 1970 to $200 by 1978, an 80.5 percent increase. The number of units renting for under $150 contracted sharply, while over 11.5-million units surged above the $200 per-month threshold.

The Changing Rental Market: Demand and Supply Interrelationships

The intersection of the demand and supply sectors of the rental market is revealed by a select, but limited, set of indicators revealing the interaction of corresponding demand and supply variables: rent-income ratios, persons per-room measures (overcrowding), and vacancy rates. Changes in these indices provide some insight into the satisfactory functioning of the housing market.

The decade of the 1970s was one in which the housing buying power of all Americans came under sustained pressures of erosion. The increasing share of the family budget that must be devoted to shelter costs has relegated to the history text older guidelines and sets of expectations, e.g., by 1980 a clear majority of all renter households expended considerably more than 25 percent of their income for rent payments. Thus, what appears to be certain levels of degeneration in the rental housing market may not be indicative of a rental housing problem *per se,* but a symbol of much more significant problems of American society. Nonetheless, while there are distressing elements, changes of a more positive kind should be noted.

1. As a result of lower income households gaining increased penetration in the rental market—in the context of steadily increasing rents—the overall median rent-income ratio shifted from 20 percent in 1970 to 25 percent by 1978.

2. This pattern of deterioration is evident across the basic profile of renter households:

Median Annual Rent as a Percent of Median Annual Income

	Total U.S. Renters		Black Central City Renters	
	1973	*1978*	*1973*	*1978*
2-or More Person Households	19.6	23.8	21.8	27.5
Male Head, Wife Present	18.2	19.4	18.1	18.2
Other Male Head	21.0	27.8	24.2	23.7
Female Head	26.9	35.8	24.9	34.1
1-Person Households	30.7	30.3	31.9	30.6

The household type with the most favorable ratios—male head, wife present (husband-wife families)—is precisely that format which is being lost to the rental market. Female headed households, as would be expected, exhibit the most ominous ratios. To reiterate, the latter represent a major growth sector in the rental market.

3. The lack of sharp differentiation between total renters and black central city renters in the preceding tabulation is mainly the result of lower rent levels attendant to the central city inventory. As has been documented previously, the latters' income resources fall far below those of their total renter counterparts.

4. While not mitigating the severity of escalating rent-income relationships, a concurrent phenomenon has been the vast reduction in overcrowding, a continuation of a trend of long-standing note. The age old vision of overcrowding while still leaving a remnant, has largely been overcome.

5. In general, vacancy rates were far lower at the end of the decade of the 1970s than at the beginning, suggesting that rental demand was growing faster than supply. However, the last two years (1979 and 1980) have seen a rise in vacancy rates, suggesting a reversal of the decade long pattern.

Homeownership: The Uncertain Alternative

An additional reference framework for viewing the deteriorating rent-income relationship is provided by the analogous financial shifts in the homeownership sector. Despite surging cost structures and obvious fiscal strictures, demand for homeownership continued to surge.

1. Between 1963 and 1970, the median sales price of new one-family homes sold in the United States increased by 30 percent; between 1970 and 1980, however, the median price soared by 186 percent. The same pattern of escalation is evidenced in the median prices of existing single-family homes sold.

2. One measure relating household income to shelter costs is the ratio of the median sales price of new one-family houses sold to median family income.

   a. Through the 1950s and 1960s, the ratio fluctuated in the vicinity of 2.9.

   b. In the early 1970s, as a result of a surge in production of federally subsidized ownership units, the ratio declined below the 2.5 level.

   c. However, by 1975, the ratio had returned to its historic benchmark, i.e., approximately 2.9. But a consistent rise was then evidenced in the ensuing years; by 1979 the sales price to income ratio reached the unprecedented level of 3.2.

3. Thus, the latter half of the 1970s witnessed a marked deterioration in the relationships between the costs of acquiring housing and income levels, a situation paralleling that of the rental market.

4. In contrast, however, the inflation in housing prices increased the demand for homeownership even with the penalty of obvious fiscal stress, a tribute to the full emergence of the post-shelter society.

It is the parallel degeneration of the renter and ownership markets that adds difficulty in projecting America's future shelter capacities in general, and rental housing's future in particular.

Issues and Dilemmas

A number of issues and considerations emanate from the preceding analyses, as well as from further investigations concerning the financing, construction, and operation of rental facilities.

1. The costs of operating rental housing have surged over the decade of the 1970s; the entire spectrum of expenditure requirements was buffeted by sustained inflation. It is difficult to envision any substantial reductions in these pressures in the 1980s, particularly in the energy cost operating components.

2. Shifts in the costs of capital (financing) have been equally severe. Renegotiable mortgages have long been used de facto in multifamily rental housing, typically written for short periods of time, though based upon long-term amortization. This permitted lending institutions to review the satisfactoriness of the payment experience as well as interest rates. While historically (pre-1970) this was a relatively passive process in terms of rates, it presently means the negotiation process is much more onerous than those accustomed to long-term fixed rate borrowing may appreciate.

3. At the same time, the limitations on expanding rents are severe. They are exacerbated, but far from limited to the constraints of rent control. Much more formidable, much more widespread, and much more chronic is the increasing paucity of rent paying capacity among the primary consumers of rental housing.

4. Thus, the substitution of government lending for multifamily rental housing purposes is in part a tribute to its availability; it also reflects on the necessity for fixed interest rates over long periods of time—and these are available only from the nonprivate sector.

5. As a result, the public sector has become not merely the lender of last resort, typically limited to the specifically impacted, but rather the primary source of multifamily rental housing finance. In the absence of such government instrumentalities, it is difficult to foresee a capacity on the part of the private market to deliver the required rental facilities.

Given these ominous trends, potential public responses must be tempered by the political potency of the long-term rental housing constituency.

Short Versus Long-Term Constitutencies

The evolving constituency for rental housing appears to be those sectors of society that cannot avail themselves of the option of homeownership—particularly the income deficient, female headed, one-parent family—as well as initial household formations. The latter—that will be increasingly centered on the "baby bust" generation as the decade of the 1980s proceeds—may elicit more immediate political sympathy and concern. However, this is a short-term temporary constituency, destined to partake of the option of home-ownership as economic and financial conditions warrant. To embark on a vast publicly supported rental housing initiative would be to replicate the school building efforts of two and one-half decades ago. If built to service a short-term clientele, the long-term problem of excess infrastructure will ultimately have to be confronted.

6. Thus, we would be hesitant to support a broad drive for the financing through governmental subvention of conventional multifamily rental structures. The longer-term demographic trends raise severe issues on the extended demand for such facilities. A much better case can be made for a continued development of facilities for the elderly—thus liberating additional housing units, both of rental and homeownership, for more youthful members of our society.

Reindustrialization Versus Housing

The price of the unparalleled pace of housing expansion in the 1970s may have been an overallocation of the nation's resource to housing. The complement of this phenomenon is envisioned as the inadequate replenishment of the nation's infrastructure and industrial base. The emergence of the concept of reindustrialization at the start of the 1980s, however vague, portends a new potential competitor for scarce resources and financial capital on a national scale. It is not difficult to foresee an analogy forming to the "guns versus butter" issue of the late 1960s. But, given the nation's economic difficulties and awareness of inflation, it may prove difficult to deliver both again. And, given the question of long-term constituencies, the political potency of rental housing may not be sufficient to render feasible a major new financial initiative.

Conversion Potential

The diminution of overcrowding in rental housing to a concern of minimal proportions is a phenomenon also characteristic of owner occupied housing. Indeed, in many cases the occupants of single-family dwellings are "overhoused"; by any measure of need, there is clearly excess shelter capacity in such instances. There is a very real potential of securing net additional rental facilities within the envelope of existing housing space.

7. Thus, a policy option is to facilitate conversion of one-family homes into two or more units. This is a process that is already taking place. It provides perhaps the least expensive and most expandable provision of rental facilities. It entirely complements the plight of the elderly homeowner faced with household chores and fiscal requirements that make ownership more and more onerous. The process is presently at work—we would recommend its advocacy and broadening through federal and local guidelines and conversion pathmarking.

Accelerating the Transition

Public policy actions that attempt a direct confrontation with powerful market forces are often doomed to failure; in many cases, the best we can hope to do is to slightly deflect those forces and/or adjust to their major thrusts. The financial and economic contours of the 1980s, particularly inflationary expectations, will probably assure the continuation of the post-shelter society. The economic necessity for homeownership will not be altered whatever expansion takes place in the rental inventory. In this context, the satisfaction of future rental housing demand may be achieved most economically by accelerating the shift from renter to owner status, i.e., the faster households that desire homeownership can achieve this goal, the faster rental facilities will be vacated for new users. Thus, facilitating the renter/owner transition via such aids as tax exempt savings plans may be an oblique way of securing rental facilities with minimal direct expenditures.

Continuing Dilemmas

As we look to the 1980s, the historical events of the late 1970s presage some immediate dilemmas. Key among these are our preliminary future demand estimates, to which we can raise serious question.

8. Employing the conventional wisdom of future household formation, as well as extrapolations of 1970 to 1980 tenure patterns, "first approximation" demand projections indicate net gains of 4.1-million renter households and 12.7-million owner households over the decade of the 1980s—growth totals comparable in magnitude to those recorded during its predecessor.

9. However, the "calibration" of the projection model is based upon a historic period of relative affluence within which rapid household formation and fragmentation were facilitated by the availability of relatively inexpensive housing. This phenomenon is not likely to be easily replicated in the coming decade; as the real costs of housing escalate, the process of household formation will decelerate.

Indeed, the latter potential will be heightened by the ominous trends in income variations and financing realities.

10. The process of income segmentation—of sharp income variations by household type and configuration—will probably accelerate over the course of the decade. While real income gains on an aggregate basis will be minimal, the reservoir of two-income households is still being filled, and represents a new partition in America's class structure. This group may well secure the affluence to board the "housing train." Conversely, a much more serious problem—obscured by the sheer size of the baby boom generation's aspirations—centers on female headed families, particularly among minority groups, whose income resources are so deficient as to be noneffective in the housing market.

11. Between these two extremes lies a population whose incomes will fail to keep pace with the costs of shelter. The basic issue is whether America can afford to provide housing at the scale and variety of configurations that we have grown to accept as our right.

12. The financing variable of the housing market equation will have to meet the challenge of alternative areas of lending and indeed of equity participation. Reindustrialization versus housing may become a confrontation of significant proportions as the nation explicitly considers whether it can afford a pattern of increased housing investment.

13. Implicitly, the demise of long-term fixed rate housing finance already serves as an indicator of emerging priorities: the costs of nonessential borrowing must be higher than the rewards. The new instrumentalities—variable rate and shared appreciation formats—serve this end, but in turn signal the reduction of housing's unique national priority.

14. The 1980s may well turn out to be an era of "shock cushioning"—of adapting the expectations of consumers to the new realities of housing costs. Whether cloaked by the euphemisms of "townhouses" or "villas," the reality will be one of masking reduced quality.

1

Housing Demand: The Evolving Profile of Rental Housing Consumers

Rental housing and its future must be viewed within the context of the sweep of national demographic events, which strongly structure both demand in the aggregate as well as its particular configurational elements. While a case can be made that the number and composition of households depends upon the availability of housing, the potency of demographic tides, within reasonable limits, is unquestionable. Thus, in order to provide baselines for estimating the future parameters of America's rental housing, it is essential that the dynamics of household compositional shifts be clearly delineated. The socioeconomic processes that are at work are manifesting themselves in very far reaching changes—their rapidity is probably without parallel in our history.

Household Compositional Shifts

The evolving profile of the nation's households throughout the 1970s has been most closely tracked by the Current Population Survey (CPS). The long-term shifts that have been recorded, particularly the heralded arrival of the maturing baby boom in the form of a flood of household formations, are presented in the data of Exhibit 1. While the total population increased by approximately 15 million between 1970 and 1979, this was overshadowed by an

EXHIBIT 1

Household Composition: 1970 and 1979
(numbers in thousands)

Subject	1970		1979		Change, 1970 to 1979		
	Number	Percent	Number	Percent	Number	Average Annual Change	Percent
All households	63,401	100.0	77,330	100.0	13,929	1,548	22.0
Family households	51,456	81.2	57,498	74.4	6,042	671	11.7
Married couple	44,728	70.5	47,662	61.6	2,934	326	6.6
No children under 18	19,196	30.3	23,157	29.9	3,961	440	20.6
With children under 18	25,532	40.3	24,505	31.7	−1,827	−114	−4.0
One-parent household	3,199	5.0	5,631	7.3	2,432	270	76.0
Lone mother with children	2,858	4.5	5,075	6.6	2,217	246	77.6
Lone father with children	341	0.5	556	0.7	215	24	63.0
Other family households	3,529	5.6	4,205	5.4	676	75	19.2
Nonfamily households	11,945	18.8	19,831	25.6	7,886	876	66.0
Persons living alone	10,851	17.1	17,201	22.2	6,350	706	58.5
Men	3,532	5.6	6,464	8.4	2,932	326	83.0
Women	7,319	11.5	10,738	13.9	3,419	380	46.7
Other nonfamily households	1,094	1.7	2,630	3.4	1,536	171	140.4

Source: U.S. Bureau of the Census *Current Population Reports,* Series P-20, no. 352, "Household and Family Characteristics: March 1979" Washington, D.C.: U.S. Government Printing Office, 1980.

incredible surge in household formation of close to 14 million, i.e., nearly one new household for every additional person added to the population.

While its antecedent was a unique birth eruption, the gains accruing to individual household types varied significantly. Married couples (husband-wife families) represented the slowest growing household type; one-parent families and nonfamily households—hitherto minor elements—the fastest. America's population is rapidly segmenting into an increasing number of varied—once considered atypical—household formats. The classic modular unit—the husband-wife family—while still dominant, is nonetheless declining in relative importance.

The ramifications of these shifts for rental housing are of vital significance. As will subsequently be shown, household income exhibits considerable variation across the range of household types. Those configurations with the greatest income resources are tending to vacate rental housing, the less affluent household types tending to predominate within it. To adequately document this phenomenon, reliance must be placed on the data secured via the *Annual Housing Survey.*

In Exhibit 2, the household compositional shifts from 1970 to 1978 (the latest *Annual Housing Survey)* are shown. While the partitions of the latter unfortunately differ from the CPS—primarily in not specifying family status—the same trends are extant. As is evident from the exhibit, the total number of households (that by definition can be synonymized with occupied housing units) increased in the seven-year period by more than one in five—21.6 percent. Within this overall increase, however, the internal variations are again clear. The classic two-or-more person household, for example, increased by a relatively modest 14.8 percent; indeed, "male head, wife present" households grew in number by less than half that rate—7.1 percent. On the other hand, one-person households increased by more than five in ten (53.9 percent) and, despite the conventional wisdom to the contrary—of the elderly being the fast growth segment in this sector—it was individuals *under* the age of sixty-five who secured the bulk of the one-person household gains.

Male and female headed households without spouse demonstrated particularly significant growth rates, 58.9 and 50.6 percent, respectively. It is noteworthy that the increase in female headed households was greater than that of "male headed, wife present" households—i.e., 3.2-million versus 3.1-million households. And, the absolute increase in one-person households was in excess of 6.0 million, far exceeding the latter totals.

Household Shifts: Rental Versus Owner Status

If we were to simply define rental housing demand in the classic conventional terms of relatively small households, the compositional shifts shown in Exhibit 2 would mandate a substantial increase in the use of such tenurial arrangements and physical configurations. But, there were other factors at work. The drive toward home-ownership, also noted earlier, expanded markedly in the 1970 to 1978 time sector, with the total number of owner occupied units (households) increasing by 26.1 percent—or nearly 10.4 million (Exhibit 3).

Again, partly as a result of the absolute increments in various sectors of the nation's demographics, the most striking ownership gains were registered by household configurations that traditionally are *not* thought of as homeowners. One-person households increased in homeownership by over 59.1 percent; even female headed house-holds had an increment in excess of one-third (44.3 percent) as did "other male headed" households (44.6 percent).

Thus, while the total number of households in America expanded by 13.7 million, 10.4 million of this total was absorbed by the owner occupied sector. Even the increase in households headed by individuals sixty-five years and over was largely devoted to owner occupancy, denying the long-term belief that the elderly would be substantially targeted into rental facilities.

Homeownership has thus expanded beyond its classic shelter role of the past. In contrast, rental housing has assumed a much more limited and much more sharply defined functional role within the United States than what held true in earlier years. This limitation in market penetration is illustrated in Exhibit 4, which details the corresponding shifts of renter households over the same time frame.

While the total number of households in the United States ex-panded by 21.6 percent, those in the rental sector grew at but two-thirds of that rate—14.1 percent. It is the compositional elements, moreover, which are most striking. The number of "male head, wife present" renter households declined by more than 2.5 million—or more than one in five over eight years. In contrast, major growth increments were one person (3.2 million) and female headed house-holds (1.8 million), typically relatively youthful ones.

These shifts are so potent as to require restatement. In Exhibit 5, a summarization has been provided, isolating the growth rates of each household configuration, further partitioned by owner and renter status. While the data only represent the surface contours of very complex processes of change—e.g., households can fragment and/or reconfigure without changing tenurial classification—a sharp

EXHIBIT 2

Total Occupied Units, Household Composition by Age of Head:
1970 and 1978
(numbers in thousands)

Household Composition by Age of Head	1970	1978	Change: 1970 to 1978	
			Number	Percent
Total Households (Occupied Units)	63,446	77,167	13,721	21.6
2-or-More-Person Households	52,295	60,009	7,714	14.8
Male Head, Wife Present	43,565	46,657	3,092	7.1
Under 25 Years	3,082	2,920	−162	−5.3
25 to 29 Years	4,660	5,362	702	15.1
30 to 34 Years	4,469	5,685	1,216	27.2
35 to 44 Years	9,251	9,515	264	2.9
45 to 64 Years	16,378	16,423	45	0.3
65 Years and Over	5,726	6,751	1,025	17.9
Other Male Head	2,441	3,879	1,438	58.9
Under 65 Years	1,984	3,395	1,411	71.1
65 Years and Over	456	485	29	6.4
Female Head	6,289	9,473	3,184	50.6
Under 65 Years	5,058	8,058	3,000	59.3
65 Years and Over	1,230	1,415	185	15.0
1-Person Households	11,151	17,158	6,007	53.9
Under 65 Years	6,184	10,032	3,848	62.2
65 Years and Over	4,967	7,124	2,157	43.4

Note: Numbers and/or percents may not add due to rounding.

Source: U.S. Department of Commerce, U.S. Bureau of the Census *Current Housing Reports*, Series H-150-78, *General Housing Characteristics for the United States and Regions: 1978*, Annual Housing Survey: 1978, Part A. Washington, D.C.: U.S. Government Printing Office, 1980.

renter/owner transition is apparent. For example, it is clear in the data that when the elderly (sixty-five years of age and over) in every configuration are isolated—or even the most youthful of the "male head, wife present" category—that the rental sector lost market penetration in areas that have been viewed as its traditional heartland: pre- and post-child rearing stages of the family life cycle.

The expansion in the use of rental facilities by "other male headed" households was 1.7 times the rate of the owner equivalent (excluding the elderly). And, while female headed configurations expanded rapidly in both sectors, renter gains outdistanced those of ownership (again, excluding the elderly). Concurrently, husband-wife (male head, wife present) units were rapidly evacuating rental facilities for homeownership tenure.

EXHIBIT 3

Owner Occupied Units, Household Composition by Age of Head:
1970 and 1978
(numbers in thousands)

Household Composition by Age of Head	1970	1978	Change: 1970 to 1978 Number	Percent
Total Owner Occupied	39,886	50,283	10,397	26.1
2-or-More-Person Households	35,124	42,708	7,584	21.6
Male Head, Wife Present	30,806	36,475	5,669	18.4
Under 25 Years	800	1,084	284	35.5
25 to 29 Years	2,252	3,170	918	40.8
30 to 34 Years	2,938	4,287	1,349	45.9
35 to 44 Years	7,097	7,879	782	11.0
45 to 64 Years	13,230	14,380	1,150	8.7
65 Years and Over	4,490	5,674	1,184	26.4
Other Male Head	1,298	1,878	580	44.6
Under 65 Years	974	1,489	515	52.9
65 Years and Over	324	390	66	20.4
Female Head	3,019	4,356	1,337	44.3
Under 65 Years	2,159	3,346	1,187	55.0
65 Years and Over	860	1,010	150	17.4
1-Person Households	4,762	7,575	2,813	59.1
Under 65 Years	2,075	3,430	1,355	65.3
65 Years and Over	2,688	4,143	1,455	54.1

Note: Numbers and/or percents may not add due to rounding.

Source: U.S. Department of Commerce, U.S. Bureau of the Census *Current Housing Reports,* Series H-150-78, *General Housing Characteristics for the United States and Regions: 1978,* Annual Housing Survey: 1978, Part A. Washington, D.C.: U.S. Government Printing Office, 1980.

Thus, increasingly, rental tenurial arrangements have become focused on nonmodular households, with the most prominent phenomenon being the movement of "male head, wife present" households from rental housing into ownership tenure. Thus, the rental market over the past decade has been "cream skimmed"— the most affluent household types have been drawn into home-ownership. This is perhaps the clearest indication of the emergence of a post-shelter society, a condition unique in its depth to our own time. Long-term chronic inflation of the duration and extent that we are undergoing alters behavior with equivalent vigor. Housing in America is much more important as a form of investment, as a form of forced savings, and as a refuge from inflation rather than from the elements. Integral to this process has been the evolving income

EXHIBIT 4

Renter Occupied Units, Household Composition by Age of Head:
1970 and 1978
(numbers in thousands)

Household Composition by Age of Head	1970	1978	Change: 1970 to 1978	
			Number	Percent
Total Renter Occupied	23,560	26,884	3,324	14.1
2-or-More-Person Households	17,171	17,301	130	0.8
Male Head, Wife Present	12,759	10,182	−2,577	−20.2
Under 25 Years	2,282	1,836	−446	−19.5
25 to 29 Years	2,408	2,192	−216	−9.0
30 to 34 Years	1,531	1,398	−133	−8.7
35 to 44 Years	2,154	1,636	−518	−24.0
45 to 64 Years	3,148	2,043	−1,105	−35.1
65 Years and Over	1,236	1,077	−159	−12.9
Other Male Head	1,143	2,001	858	75.1
Under 65 Years	1,010	1,906	896	88.7
65 Years and Over	132	95	−37	−28.0
Female Head	3,270	5,117	1,847	56.5
Under 65 Years	2,899	4,712	1,813	62.5
65 Years and Over	370	405	35	9.5
1-Person Households	6,389	9,583	3,194	50.0
Under 65 Years	4,109	6,602	2,493	60.7
65 Years and Over	2,279	2,981	702	30.8

Note: Numbers and/or percents may not add due to rounding.

Source: U.S. Department of Commerce, U.S. Bureau of the Census *Current Housing Reports,* Series H-150-78, *General Housing Characteristics for the United States and Regions: 1978,* Annual Housing Survey: 1978, Part A. Washington, D.C.: U.S. Government Printing Office, 1980.

realities over the past decade. It is, however, appropriate at this stage to focus on a major sector that epitomizes the renter compositional shifts: black central city tenants.

The Black Central City Renter Household

In Exhibit 6, data on the shift that has taken place from 1970 to 1978 in the profile of black central city renter households are summarized. The absolute number of such households increased by one in five (22.3 percent). The latter rate, however, was virtually double that of "two-or-more-person" households. But, most significantly, the number of black central city husband-wife renter households declined by fully 24.9 percent—or nearly one in four.

EXHIBIT 5

Owner and Renter Occupied Units, Change in Household Composition by Age of Head: 1970 and 1978

Household Composition by Age of Head	Total	Renter	Owner
Total Households	21.6%	14.1%	26.1%
2-or-More-Person Households	14.8	0.8	21.6
Male Head, Wife Present	7.1	−20.2	18.4
Under 25 Years	−5.3	−19.5	35.5
25 to 29 Years	15.1	−9.0	40.8
30 to 34 Years	27.2	−8.7	45.9
35 to 44 Years	2.9	−24.0	11.0
45 to 64 Years	0.3	−35.1	8.7
65 Years and Over	17.9	−12.9	26.4
Other Male Head	58.9	75.1	44.6
Under 65 Years	71.1	88.7	52.9
65 Years and Over	6.4	−28.0	20.4
Female Head	50.6	56.5	44.3
Under 65 Years	59.3	62.5	55.0
65 Years and Over	15.0	9.5	17.4
1-Person Households	53.9	50.0	59.1
Under 65 Years	62.2	60.7	65.3
65 Years and Over	43.4	30.8	54.1

Note: Numbers and/or percents may not add due to rounding.

Source: U.S. Department of Commerce, U.S. Bureau of the Census, *Current Housing Reports*, Series H-150-78, *General Housing Characteristics for the United States and Regions: 1978*, Annual Housing Survey: 1978, Part A. Washington, D.C.: U.S. Government Printing Office, 1980.

While this was most striking in the more youthful sectors, it extended across the age spectrum.

The contrast of the latter shrinkage with the expansion of female headed households—56.9 percent—is particularly striking; and this in turn was nearly matched by the 54.9 percent increment in black one-person households.

Thus, while black renter households in central cities expanded by more than one-half million over eight years, there was an absolute loss in "male head, wife present" configurations of a quarter of a million. At the same time, female headed households expanded in number by 414,000, while an additional increment in excess of 340,000 was registered in one-person households.

The increasing skew in distribution in the profiles of black central city renter households is emphasized by their comparison to the

EXHIBIT 6

Black Central City Renter Household Composition Shift
by Age of Head:
1970 and 1978
(numbers in thousands)

Household Composition by Age of Head	1970	1978	Change: 1970 to 1978	
			Number	Percent
Total Households	2,498	3,055	557	22.3
2-or-More-Person Households	1,868	2,079	211	11.3
Male Head, Wife Present	1,003	753	−250	−24.9
Under 25 Years	138	79	−59	−42.8
25 to 29 Years	174	148	−26	−14.9
30 to 34 Years	140	97	−43	−30.7
35 to 44 Years	212	160	−52	−24.5
45 to 64 Years	259	196	−63	−24.3
65 Years and Over	79	73	−6	−7.6
Other Male Head	137	185	48	35.0
Under 65 Years	120	173	53	44.2
65 Years and Over	17	12	−5	−29.4
Female Head	727	1,141	414	56.9
Under 65 Years	679	1,088	409	60.2
65 Years and Over	48	53	5	10.4
1-Person Households	630	976	346	54.9
Under 65 Years	476	744	268	56.3
65 Years and Over	154	232	78	50.6

Note: Numbers and/or percents may not add due to rounding.

Source: U.S. Department of Commerce, U.S. Bureau of the Census *Current Housing Reports*, Series H-150-78, *General Housing Characteristics for the United States and Regions: 1978*, Annual Housing Survey: 1978, Part A. Washington, D.C.: U.S. Government Printing Office, 1980.

corresponding distributions for the nation's total households as well as all renter households (Exhibit 7). While the incidence of two or more person households in both rental sectors is roughly comparable, only one in four (24.6 percent) central city black renter households is of the "male head, wife present" format in contrast to nearly four in ten (37.9 percent) of all renter households. Even more distinctive is the variation in female headed households—the incidence rate for all of the nation's households is but one-third that of central city black renter households (12.3 versus 37.4 percent). Indeed, the latter incidence is twice that of all U.S. renters (19.0 percent). Thus, while rental households in total have experienced considerable withdrawals of husband-wife configurations, and a growing presence of female headed households, the central city

EXHIBIT 7

Total U.S., Total U.S. Renter, and Central City Black Renter
Households, by Configuration
1970 and 1978
(Percent Distribution)

Household Configuration	Total U.S. Households		Total U.S. Renter Households		Central City Black Renter Households	
	1970	1978	1970	1978	1970	1978
TOTAL HOUSEHOLDS	100.0	100.0	100.0	100.0	100.0	100.0
2-or-More Person Households	82.4	77.8	72.9	64.4	74.7	68.1
Male Head, Wife Present	68.7	60.5	54.1	37.9	40.1	24.6
Other Male Head	3.8	5.0	4.9	7.4	5.5	6.1
Female Head	9.9	12.3	13.9	19.0	29.1	37.4
1-Person Households	17.6	22.2	27.1	35.6	25.2	31.9

Source: U.S. Department of Commerce, U.S. Bureau of the Census, *Current Housing Reports*, Series H-150-78, *General Housing Characteristics for the United States and Regions, 1978*, Annual Housing Survey: 1978, Part A. Washington, D.C.: U.S. Government Printing Office, 1980.

black renter population represents the extreme edge of this phenomenon. By 1978, female headed households evolved into the dominant (37.4 percent of total) sector of the black central city rental market. The housing policy ramifications of this dynamic trendline are further accentuated as income variations are scrutinized.

The Renter Income Dilemma

The necessity for rent increases in a time of inflation—not least as a consequence of the cost of money—is all too evident. The limitations, however, are largely related to the lagging fiscal capacity of renters. In this section, the income shifts that have characterized the respective pools of owners and renters are examined in some detail.

The broad picture of income changes in the United States from 1970 to 1979 is illustrated in Exhibit 8. The two basic household sectors as defined by the CPS comprise families and unrelated individuals. While the incomes of the latter grew at a rapid pace, in the terminal year (1979) their income was a very modest $7,542; family income, on the other hand, was well above the $19,000 mark ($19,684). Within the family grouping, however, there were enormously potent variations. Thus, married couple families with wives in the paid labor force had median incomes of nearly $25,000 by

EXHIBIT 8

Median Income by Family Type, U.S. Total: 1970 to 1979

Household Type	1970	1979	Change: 1970 to 1979	
			Number	Percent
Total Families	$ 9,867	$19,684	$ 9,817	99.5%
Married Couple Families	10,516	21,521	11,005	104.7
Wife in Paid Labor Force	12,276	24,973	12,697	103.4
Wife not in Paid Labor Force	9,304	17,791	8,487	91.2
Male Households, No Wife Present	9,012	16,888	7,876	87.4
Female Households, No Husband Present	5,093	9,933	4,840	95.0
Unrelated Individuals	3,137	7,542	4,405	140.5

All Families	1970	1979	Change: 1970 to 1979	
			Number	Percent
Renter	$ 9,775	$12,704	$2,929	30.0%
Owner	15,464	22,077	6,613	42.8

Source: U.S. Bureau of the Census, *Current Population Reports*, Series P-60, no. 125, *Money Income and Poverty Status of Families and Persons in the United States: 1979* (Advanced Report) Washington, D.C.: Government Printing Office, 1980.

1979, while equivalent configurations with wives not in the paid labor force were still below the $18,000 mark. Demonstrating significant lags were female householders (with no husband present) whose incomes were below $10,000. Both in terms of percentage growth as well as absolute scale, it is married couple families that showed the greatest levels of increased affluence in the 1970s.

One implication of this phenomenon to the broader housing market is detailed in the lower portions of Exhibit 8. In 1975, families in rental housing had incomes slightly under the $10,000 mark, less than two-thirds that of owners ($15,464). By 1979, renter incomes had increased by 30.0 percent to $12,704. The income of owners, however, grew to $22,077, a rate of increase of 42.8 percent, indicating a substantially widening gap. This pattern is not the result of variations in the income of a constant set of families over time—household transfers between the pools of renters and owners is the more potent dynamic. The more affluent of the former, given the tax and inflation shelters attendant to ownership, shift into that status; those who cannot afford homeownership remain in the renter pool.

EXHIBIT 9

Owner and Renter Occupied Household Income,
by Household Configuration,
U.S. Total: 1973

Household Composition by Age of Head	Owner Occupied	Renter Occupied	Renter/ Owner Ratio
Total Households	$11,500	$ 7,200	.63
2-or-More-Person Households	12,600	8,600	.68
Male Head, Wife Present	13,000	9,500	.73
Under 25 Years	9,800	8,300	.85
25 to 29 Years	12,600	10,700	.83
30 to 34 Years	14,100	10,900	.77
35 to 44 Years	14,900	10,800	.72
45 to 64 Years	14,100	10,400	.74
65 Years and Over	6,100	4,900	.80
Other Male Head	12,500	8,600	.69
Under 65 Years	13,600	9,000	.66
65 Years and Over	7,400	4,800	.65
Female Head	8,000	5,800	.73
Under 65 Years	8,700	5,900	.68
65 Years and Over	6,100	4,600	.75
1-Person Households	4,000	4,500	1.13
Under 65 Years	6,300	6,200	.98
65 Years and Over	3,000—	3,000—	—

Note: Numbers and/or percents may not add due to rounding.

Source: U.S. Department of Commerce, U.S. Bureau of the Census, *Current Housing Reports,* Series H-150-73, *General Housing Characteristics for the United States and Regions: 1973,* Annual Housing Survey: 1973, Part A. Washington, D.C.: U.S. Government Printing Office, 1974.

The potent blending of demographic/income characteristics and their linkage to tenurial status is further illustrated in Exhibits 9 and 10, which show owner and renter household income by household configuration for 1973 and 1978 (the last year of the *Annual Housing Survey* that is presently available). As is evident from the exhibits, there has been a significant deterioration in renter incomes relative to their owner counterparts for every household configuration. This phenomenon is most accentuated in the case of female headed households. In 1973, such households who rented had 73 percent of the median incomes of those who owned their own facilities. By 1978, the ratio deteriorated to 57 percent. And, as has been previously shown, the female headed household is one of the fastest

EXHIBIT 10

Owner and Renter Occupied Household Income,
by Household Configuration,
U.S. Total: 1978

Household Composition by Age of Head	Total Owner Occupied	Total Renter Occupied	Renter/ Owner Ratio
Total Households	$16,800	$ 9,300	.55
2-or-More-Person Households	18,900	10,900	.58
Male Head, Wife Present	20,000	13,700	.69
Under 25 Years	14,900	11,900	.80
25 to 29 Years	19,200	14,400	.75
30 to 34 Years	21,200	15,900	.75
35 to 44 Years	23,200	16,000	.69
45 to 64 Years	22,200	14,400	.65
65 Years and Over	10,000	8,100	.81
Other Male Head	16,300	10,200	.63
Under 65 Years	17,600	10,400	.59
65 Years and Over	11,200	8,100	.72
Female Head	11,600	6,600	.57
Under 65 Years	12,100	6,600	.55
65 Years and Over	10,000	6,600	.66
1-Person Households	6,600	6,900	1.05
Under 65 Years	10,700	9,300	.87
65 Years and Over	5,100	4,500	.88

Note: Numbers and/or Percents may not add due to rounding.

Source: U.S. Department of Commerce, U.S. Bureau of the Census, *Current Housing Reports*, Series H-150-78, *General Housing Characteristics for the United States and Regions: 1978*, Annual Housing Survey: 1978, Part A. Washington, D.C.: U.S. Government Printing Office, 1980.

growing sectors of the rental housing market. The renter household type most competitive in terms of income and that has shown the least erosion in relative income over time, is the husband-wife (male head, wife present) category. However, this is the group that is disappearing most rapidly from renter tenure.

The Problem of Black Central City Renter Households

The issues of income competence with which to cope with escalating rent levels are most accentuated when the focus is on black center city renter households. This is illustrated in Exhibits 11 and 12, which detail household income by household configuration for

EXHIBIT 11

Renter Occupied Household Income, by Household Configuration,
U.S. Total and Central City Black Households: 1973

Household Composition by Age of Head	U.S. Renter Total	Central City Black Renter Households	Black Renter/ Total Renter Ratio
Total Households	$ 7,200	$ 5,800	.81
2-or-More-Person Households	8,600	6,500	.76
Male Head, Wife Present	9,500	8,400	.88
Under 25 Years	8,300	8,700	1.05
25 to 29 Years	10,700	9,700	.91
30 to 34 Years	10,900	10,600	.97
35 to 44 Years	10,800	8,400	.78
45 to 64 Years	10,400	6,800	.65
65 Years and Over	4,900	3,100	.63
Other Male Head	8,600	5,900	.69
Under 65 Years	9,000	6,300	.70
65 Years and Over	4,800	—	—
Female Head	5,800	5,300	.91
Under 65 Years	5,900	5,400	.92
65 Years and Over	4,600	4,400	.96
1-Person Households	4,500	3,500	.78

Note: Numbers and/or percents may not add due to rounding.

Source: U.S. Department of Commerce, U.S.Bureau of the Census, *Current Housing Reports,* Series H-150-73, *General Housing Characteristics for the United States and Regions: 1973,* Annual Housing Survey: 1973, Part A. Washington, D.C.: U.S. Government Printing Office, 1974.

the total rental population—versus that of central city black renters for 1973 and 1978, respectively. In the former year, the income of all black central city renter households was 81 percent of that of all renter households; by 1978 the ratio had declined to 70 percent. However, while this deterioration can in no way be minimized, it has been caused mainly by the minimal income gains accruing to female headed households and one-person households, the two groups bulking largest in the black central city renter profile (see Exhibit 6). In contrast, the improving position of the "male head, wife present" format has minimal overall impact, since it is a group rapidly being depleted from the black renter market in the central city. This is the subgroup that has been most able to avail itself of the alternative of homeownership (as well as suburban location).

EXHIBIT 12

Renter Occupied Household Income, by Household Configuration,
U.S. Total and Central City Black Households: 1978

Household Composition by Age of Head	U.S. Renter Total	Central City Black Renter Households	Black Renter/ Total Renter Ratio
Total Households	$ 9,300	$ 6,500	.70
2-or-More-Person Households	10,900	7,500	.69
Male Head, Wife Present	13,700	12,300	.90
Under 25 Years	11,900	11,000	.92
25 to 29 Years	14,400	13,300	.92
30 to 34 Years	15,900	13,500	.85
35 to 44 Years	16,000	14,700	.92
45 to 64 Years	14,400	12,200	.85
65 Years and Over	8,100	6,000	.74
Other Male Head	10,200	9,300	.91
Under 65 Years	10,400	9,800	.94
65 Years and Over	8,100	—	—
Female Head	6,600	5,600	.85
Under 65 Years	6,600	5,500	.83
65 Years and Over	6,600	7,100	1.08
1-Person Households	6,900	5,300	.77

Note: Numbers and/or percents may not add due to rounding.

Source: U.S. Department of Commerce, U.S. Bureau of the Census, *Current Housing Reports*, Series H-150-78, *General Housing Characteristics for the United States and Regions: 1978*, Annual Housing Survey: 1978, Part A. Washington, D.C.: U.S. Government Printing Office, 1980.

The total renter/owner income ratios and the black central city renter/total renter income ratios are summarized in Exhibit 13 for the purposes of clarification of the dynamics at work. It is readily apparent that the growth segments of rental demand are those households least equipped fiscally to support rent increases. Rental housing in terms of market penetration has strikingly lost its appeal to the more affluent—increasingly it is the abode of those with limited housing buying power. The process is most strikingly advanced among black households; particularly those which are female headed.

EXHIBIT 13

Summary: Income Ratios

Household Composition by Age of Head	1973 Renter/ Owner Ratio	1978 Renter/ Owner Ratio	1973 Black Renter/ Total Renter Ratio	1978 Black Renter/ Total Renter Ratio
Total Households	.63	.55	.81	.70
2-or-More-Person Households	.68	.58	.76	.69
Male Head, Wife Present	.73	.69	.88	.90
Under 25 Years	.85	.80	1.05	.92
25 to 29 Years	.83	.75	.91	.92
30 to 34 Years	.77	.75	.97	.85
35 to 44 Years	.72	.69	.78	.92
45 to 64 Years	.74	.65	.65	.85
65 Years and Over	.80	.81	.63	.74
Other Male Head	.69	.63	.69	.91
Under 65 Years	.66	.59	.70	.94
65 Years and Over	.65	.72	—	—
Female Head	.73	.57	.91	.85
Under 65 Years	.68	.55	.92	.83
65 Years and Over	.75	.66	.96	1.08
1-Person Households	1.13	1.05	.78	.77
Under 65 Years	.98	.87	—	—
65 Years and Over	—	.88	—	—

Source: U.S. Department of Commerce, U.S. Bureau of the Census, *Current Housing Reports*, Series H-150-78, *General Housing Characteristics for the United States and Regions: 1978*, Annual Housing Survey: 1978, Part A. Washington, D.C.: U.S. Government Printing Office, 1980.

Summary

1. A major determinant of housing demand is the evolution of both the number and composition of the nation's households. Between 1970 and 1979, the total number of households increased by almost 14 million, an increment comparable to that of the growth in total population (approximately 15 million people) for the corresponding time interval.

2. The gains accruing to individual household types varied significantly, however. Husband-wife configurations represented the slowest growing household type, one-parent families and nonfamily households the fastest. America's population

is rapidly partitioning itself into an increasing number of varied, once considered "atypical," household arrangements.

3. When changing household profiles are sectored by tenure, sharp differentials are evident between owner and renter occupied sectors. Over the 1970 to 1978 time period, the following trends were operative:

   a. Of the total gains in owner households (10.9 million), 5.7 million were husband-wife configurations.

   b. The second largest growth sector comprised one-person households (2.8 million). However, the rate of increase (59.1 percent) of the latter was more than triple that of husband-wife households (18.4 percent).

   c. While "other male head" and "female head" configurations experienced smaller absolute growth increments, their rates of increase (44.6 and 44.3 percent, respectively) were also far greater than that registered by husband-wife households.

4. The rental sector, over the 1970 to 1978 period, exhibited tendencies of a substantially different nature:

   a. While the total number of renter households increased by 3.3 million, a loss of 2.6 million husband-wife renter households was concurrently experienced (-20.2 percent).

   b. One-person households, in contrast, increased by 3.2 million, or 50.0 percent. The growth rates for "other male head" (75.1 percent) and "female head" (56.5 percent) configurations were even higher, but their absolute growth increments were somewhat smaller in magnitude.

5. As a result of these household shifts, rental housing has assumed a much more limited and much more sharply defined functional role within the United States than held true in earlier years. With the declining presence of husband-wife households, rental facilities have become increasingly focused on nonmodular households. The rental sector has lost market penetration in areas that have been viewed as its traditional heartland—pre- and post-child rearing stages of the family life cycle.

6. When black central city renter households are isolated, the preceding phenomena are even more accentuated. While the

number of husband-wife formats declined by one in four (24.9 percent) in the rental sector, female headed households increased by 56.9 percent and one-person households by 55 percent. By 1978, female headed households evolved into the dominant (37.4 percent of total) sector of the black central city rental market. The following profiles illustrate the overall contours of the phenomena:

Household Configuration	Total U.S. Households 1970	1978	Total U.S. Renter Households 1970	1978	Central City Black Renter Households 1970	1978
TOTAL HOUSEHOLDS	100.0	100.0	100.0	100.0	100.0	100.0
2-or-More Person Households	82.4	77.8	72.9	64.4	74.7	68.1
Male Head, Wife Present	68.7	60.5	54.1	37.9	40.1	24.6
Other Male Head	3.8	5.0	4.9	7.4	5.5	6.1
Female Head	9.9	12.3	13.9	19.0	29.1	37.4
1-Person Households	17.6	22.2	27.1	35.6	25.2	31.9

7. Attendant to the changing profile of renter/owner household configurations are sharp distinctions in fiscal capacities and income levels. Husband-wife configurations, particularly when the wife is in the paid labor force, is the most affluent household type; however, it is this precise market sector that is vacating rental housing. Female and male headed households without spouse, and one-person households, are characterized by much lower income resources; these are the household types that are increasingly dominating the rental market.

8. The following income ratios are illustrative of the income differentials that are developing:

Household Configuration	1973 Renter/ Owner Ratio	1978 Renter/ Owner Ratio	1973 Black Renter/ Total Renter Ratio	1978 Black Renter/ Total Renter Ratio
TOTAL HOUSEHOLDS	.63	.55	.88	.70
2-or-More Person Households	.68	.58	.76	.69
Male Head, Wife Present	.73	.69	.88	.90
Other Male Head	.69	.63	.69	.91
Female Head	.73	.57	.91	.85
1-Person Households	1.13	1.09	.78	.77

By 1978, the income of all renter households was only 55 percent of owner income; concurrently, the income of black central city renters was only 70 percent of that of all renter households. The most competitive renter income household— male head, wife present—is rapidly withdrawing from rental tenure. This is particularly the case for the black central city sector.

2

Preliminary Estimates of
Future Housing Demand:
Owner Versus Rental

Establishing the Base: The Limitations of the Data Sources

There are two principal data sources that detail basic household
totals and general characteristics. Unfortunately, the two are far
from completely compatible in terms of demographic partitions.
As indicated in Exhibit 1, the *Annual Housing Survey* (AHS) does
not detail family status to the degree of the *Current Population
Survey* (CPS), which utilizes family/nonfamily classification as its
primary partitioning device. This variation creates difficulties in
projecting future demand by renter and owner status, since the
CPS provides projections of future household totals by type and
configuration, while the AHS provides the basis for establishing
future tenure (rental versus owner) shares according to household
configuration. In order to link the household projections of the
CPS to the historical tenure parameters securable via the AHS,
a common household definitional format is required. The latter
is indicated in the bottom of Exhibit 1. Each of the data sources
can be reconfigured into a compatible format via these partitions.

In the act of providing a common denominator for the two
definitional approaches, much in the way of detail is lost; however,
the result does provide a basis for estimating future demand. The

36

EXHIBIT 1

Alternative Household Partitions

		Component Identification
Annual Housing Survey (AHS)		
Household Partitions		
2-or-More-Person Households		
Male Head, Wife Present		1
Other Male Head		2
Female Head		3
1-Person Households		
Male Head		4
Female Head		5
Current Population Survey (CPS)		
Household Partitions		
Family Households		
Husband-Wife		A
Male Householder, No Wife Present		B
Female Householder, No Husband Present		C
Nonfamily Households		
Male		D
Female		E

Common Format (Reconfigured)
Household Partitions

	Components	
Configuration	*AHS*	*CPS*
Male Head, Wife Present	1	A
Male Head, Other	2+4	B+D
Female Head, Other	3+5	C+E

three groupings that are utilized in the material that follows are thus labeled "male head, wife present;" "male head, other;" and "female head, other." The component identification numbers and letters indicate the composition of each of the groupings.

The Changing Historical Pattern

Despite the limitations of extrapolation, projections depend upon a strong grasp of the antecedents of the phenomena under study. Therefore, Exhibit 2 recaps the owner/renter status of the nation's households for 1970 and 1977, based upon the AHS, recalibrated into the common format. The pattern is one that is very familiar—

EXHIBIT 2

Renter and Owner Status, By Household
Partition (Common Format), U.S. Total, 1970 and 1977
(numbers in thousands)

	1970		
	Owners	*Renter*	*Total*
TOTAL	39,885	23,561	63,446
Male Head, Wife Present	30,806	12,759	43,565
Male Head, Other	2,627	3,747	6,374
Female Head, Other	6,452	7,055	13,507
	Percent Distribution		
TOTAL	62.9	37.1	100.0
Male Head, Wife Present	70.7	29.3	100.0
Male Head, Other	41.2	58.8	100.0
Female Head, Other	47.8	52.2	100.0
	1977		
TOTAL	48,765	26,515	75,280
Male Head, Wife Present	36,274	10,748	47,022
Male Head, Other	3,763	5,991	9,754
Female Head, Other	8,728	9,776	18,504
	Percent Distribution		
TOTAL	64.8	35.2	100.0
Male Head, Wife Present	77.1	22.9	100.0
Male Head, Other	38.6	61.4	100.0
Female Head, Other	47.2	52.8	100.0

Source: U.S. Department of Commerce, U.S. Bureau of the Census. *Current Housing Reports,* Series H-150-77, *General Housing Characteristics for the United States and Regions: 1977,* Annual Housing Survey: 1977, Part A. Washington, D.C.: U.S. Government Printing Office, 1979.

of homeownership increasing in dominance among "male head, wife present" households. By 1977, it accounted for more than three-quarters (77.1 percent) of such households, in contrast to 70.7 percent in 1970. The other two configurations shown are relatively static in terms of their tenurial shifts with renter occupancy gaining slightly. By 1977, fully three-quarters of all owners were "male head, wife present" households; barely one-sixth were female headed.

The situation differs however, when rental housing is considered. "Male head, wife present" households comprise fewer than 40

EXHIBIT 3

Projected Owner-Renter Shares
Selected Household Configurations

	1970	*1977*	*1980*	*1990*
Male Head, Wife Present				
Owner	70.7	77.1	79.4	86.9
Renter	29.3	22.9	20.6	13.1
Male Head, Other				
Owner	41.2	38.6	37.6	33.9
Renter	58.8	61.4	62.4	66.1
Female Head, Other				
Owner	47.8	47.2	46.9	46.1
Renter	52.2	52.8	53.1	53.9

Source: CUPR Projections and Exhibit 2.

percent of all renters—a percentage that is nearly matched by female households.

Projected Owner/Renter Shares

The precise share of the market that will be secured by the two tenurial forms in the future clearly is subject to a vast complex of forces: financial, economic, sociological, and political, among many others. For the purposes of illustration, however, presented in Exhibit 3 is a simple linear extrapolation to 1980 and 1990 of the trends indicated by the historical 1970 to 1977 experience. By 1990, 86.9 percent of "male head, wife present" households are projected to be owners. "Other male headed" households will have declined in ownership tenure to slightly more than one-third (33.3 percent). "Female head, other" households demonstrate relative stability, with ownership tenure declining from 47.2 percent to 46.1 percent over the 1977 to 1990 period.

Within the comparative coarseness of the demographic groupings to which we are limited, there are subsectors with varying income and tenure trends. However, despite the potential heterogeneity of the categories, they can serve as a baseline for broad approximation.

If the focus is on rental housing, it should be reiterated (even at the risk of redundancy) that America's higher income households are diminishing as occupants of rental facilities. As shown in Exhibit 3, for example, "male head, wife present" households are the fastest "outmovers." One out of five (20.6 percent) of such households in 1980 occupy rental facilities; by 1990, there is close to a 40-percent decline to barely one in eight (13.1 percent). Thus, rental housing is left increasingly to the two sectors of lowest income—and thus with the most limited rent paying capacities.

Projections of Future Households by Configuration

The above section has attempted to define future market penetration of owner and rental tenure by household configuration. But what is the future magnitude of each of the household types? Exhibit 4 presents both historical data (1970 and 1979) as well as projections (1980 and 1990) from the CPS. Clearly, the decade of the 1980s, from a demographic perspective, will be somewhat different from its predecessor. The aging of the baby boom—and the significance of the baby bust that has followed—are mirrored in the data. From 1970 to 1979, for example, the absolute growth of nonfamily households was twice that of husband-wife families. The growth of "female households, no husband present" (2.7 million) was within 75 percent of the 3.6-million increase of husband-wife families.

In contrast, the dominant growth sector of the 1980s comprises husband-wife configurations, which are projected to gain 5.7-million families, or more than half again the absolute growth increment of the previous decade. While nonfamily households have a far higher *rate of increase,* their absolute growth increment is comparable to that of the previous decade. The same holds basically true for "female householders, no husband present," whose gain of 2.9 million is half that of the husband-wife format.

Thus, the decade of the 1980s is one in which the growth in total household numbers will exceed that secured in the 1970s. But, bulking larger in the projected totals are husband-wife configurations, at least in comparison to the past decade.

The linkage of these projections to the tenure extrapolations necessitates reformating to the partitions of Exhibit 1, which alters the growth patterns. This is detailed in Exhibit 5. Husband-wife households in the 1980s, as discussed above, will increase in number by nearly 5.7 million; "male head, other" by approximately 4.6 million; and "female head, other" by more than 6.4 million. By 1990, this last group, typically characterized by lower incomes, will be fully half the equivalent number of husband-wife households.

EXHIBIT 4

Household Shifts, by Configuration
U.S. Total: 1970 to 1979 and 1980 to 1990
(numbers in thousands)

	1970	1979	Change: 1970 to 1979 Number	Percent
Total Households	63,450	77,330	13,880	21.9%
Family Households				
Husband-Wife	44,062	47,662	3,600	8.2
Male Householder, No Wife Present	1,402	1,616	214	15.3
Female Householder, No Husband Present	5,504	8,220	2,716	49.3
Nonfamily Households				
Male	4,631	8,064	3,433	74.1
Female	7,850	11,767	3,917	49.9

	1980	1990	Change: 1980 to 1990 Number	Percent
Total Households	79,870	96,653	16,783	21.0%
Family Households				
Husband-Wife	48,968	54,731	5,763	11.7
Male Householder, No Wife Present	1,657	2,181	524	31.6
Female Householder, No Husband Present	8,611	11,572	2,961	34.4
Nonfamily Householders				
Male	8,613	12,689	4,076	47.3
Female	12,022	15,477	3,455	28.7

Note: Projections are New Series B.

Source: U.S. Bureau of the Census, *Current Population Reports,* Series P-20, no. 352, "Household and Family Characteristics: March 1979." Washington, D.C.: U.S. Government Printing Office, 1980. U.S. Bureau of the Census, *Current Population Reports,* Series P-25, no. 805, "Projections of the Numbers of Households and Families: 1979 to 1995." Washington, D.C.: U.S. Government Printing Office, 1979.

Linking Demographic Projections to Housing Tenure

The product of the corresponding tenure (Exhibit 3) and household (Exhibit 5) projections is shown in Exhibit 6. The bottom of the exhibit summarizes the levels of growth forecast for total owner and renter demand given a consistency of trendline. Between 1980 and 1990, an additional 12.7-million households (24.1 percent) will be seeking homeownership. Over the same period, 4.1-million households will be requiring rental accommodations.

EXHIBIT 5

Reconfigured Household Projections,
U.S. Total: 1980 and 1990
(numbers in thousands)

	Original	
	1980	*1990*
Total Households	79,870	96,653
Family Households		
Husband-Wife	48,968	54,731
Male Householder, No Wife Present	1,657	2,185
Female Householder, No Husband Present	8,611	11,572
Nonfamily Households		
Male	8,613	12,689
Female	12,022	15,477
	Reconfigured	
	1980	*1990*
Total Households	79,870	96,653
Husband-Wife	48,968	54,731
Male Head, Other	10,270	14,874
Female Head, Other	20,633	27,049

Note: Numbers may not add due to rounding.
Source: See Exhibits 1 and 4.

An examination of the upper portions of Exhibit 6 reveals substantial changes of tenure by each household type. For example, while an additional 8.7-million "male head, wife present" households are projected to desire owner occupied facilities, there is a projected decline of 2.9 million in the rental sector. Both "male head, other" and "female head, other" configurations dominate the increment in the number of renter households, with each accounting for a growth of approximately 3.5 million. The sum of their ownership demand, however, is less than half that of the "male head, wife present" sector. Thus, two-thirds of the projected ownership growth comprises "male head, wife present" households, but so significant are the shifts in tenure form that literally 150 percent of the rental demand emerges from the other two household configurations.

EXHIBIT 6

Owner/Renter Household Projections:
1980 to 1990
(numbers in thousands)

	1980	1990	Change: 1980 to 1990	
			Number	Percent
Male Head, Wife Present	48,968	54,731	—	—
Owner	38,881	47,561	8,680	22.3
Renter	10,087	7,170	−2,917	−28.9
Male Head, Other	10,270	14,874	—	—
Owner	3,862	5,042	1,180	30.6
Renter	6,408	9,832	3,424	53.4
Female Head, Other	20,633	27,049	—	—
Owner	9,677	12,470	2,793	28.9
Renter	10,956	14,579	3,623	33.1
TOTAL OWNER	52,420	65,073	12,653	24.1
TOTAL RENTER	27,451	31,581	4,130	15.0
Total	79,871	96,654	16,783	21.0

Source: CUPR Projections.

Some Perspective on the Projections

Are the projections of housing demand shown here indicative of abrupt discontinuities in long-term trendlines? Or, rather do they represent numbers that are well within the mainstream of our experience? While neither of these conditions is in itself a certification of their accuracy, certainly the latter is far more reassuring than the former. Within this context, as shown in Exhibit 7, it is noteworthy that the growth of the renter and owner sectors is well within the historic mainstream. From 1970 to 1977, an average annual change in renter households of 422,000 was experienced. The corresponding annual increment in the 1980 to 1990 projection period was 413,000. The real stress on the housing market of the 1980s will continue to emanate from ownership demand whose annual change will remain in the vicinity of 1.3-million households.

But, is this a realistic vision of the housing economy to come? The problems of forecasting are never easy, but certainly are as difficult at this moment of time as they have ever been. The basic issue is whether America can afford to provide housing at the scale

EXHIBIT 7

Average Annual Changes, Renter and Owner Households:
1970 to 1977 and 1980 to 1990
(numbers in thousands)

	Change: 1970 to 1977	Average Annual Change
Renter Households	2,954	422
Owner Households	8,880	1,269
	Change: 1980 to 1990	Average Annual Change
Renter Households	4,130	413
Owner Households	12,653	1,265

Source: See Exhibits 2 and 6.

and variety of configurations that we have grown to accept as our right.

Depth of the Two-Income Reservoir: Income Capacities

The growing imbalance between consumer housing buying power and the cost of ownership has been adequately documented. The bridges between these incomes and costs, as earlier referred to, have been the subsidies available through preferential tax treatment and, even more strikingly, of inflationary expectation. Added to these in the last several years have been a variety of new or renovated financing mechanisms that at least have given the appearance of providing greater access to the market for groups that otherwise would be priced out of the competition.

Equally striking has been the growth of the two-income household. One of the new major economic class structures of America is the partition between one-income and two-income households. And the processes at work in this sector are far from complete. While it has often been stressed that over half of all married women are now in the labor force—implicitly suggesting that the capacity for future household income growth via this phenomenon is approaching its limits—delving further into the labor statistics reveals a more salient reality: *only 17 percent of all husband-wife households have both members working full time year round.* Thus, the reservoir of two-income households, upon which much of the *effective* demand for housing is and will be based, is far from exhausted. Substantial additions can be expected in light of anticipated demographic trendlines.

Problem Sectors: Female Headed Families

Outside of this relatively secure segment, however, remains the major problem of housing as shelter—the issue of those who cannot afford anything close to real market requirements. Dominant in this context is the rise of the female headed family, particularly among minority groups.

As detailed in the preceding chapter, this is one of the weakest incomed sectors within the overall demographic fabric of America, as well as one of the fastest growing. Its growing preponderance in rental housing is one of the direct causes of the problems that are being experienced in that segment of the housing market. The income levels that are shown reflect the incompetence of buying power to meet the real cost structures of even minimal housing. Unless very basic organic changes are made in family patterns, it is this group that will need increased public subsidization.

What then of the housing forecasts for the 1980s? We would suggest very strongly that projected rates of household formation that utilize historic patterning may unduly reflect past periods of relative affluence—most of all in real housing costs. Households have been able to undouble (or perhaps, unkindly, to split) because of the availability of housing at relatively inexpensive prices. When the real cost of housing goes up, this process will slow down. If we were to reach a real depression, based upon historic evidence, this phenomenon would be reversed, i.e., yielding a reduction in number of households for a finite population. There is some indication that this process is already at work.

Summary

1. Recalibrating the *Annual Housing Survey* (AHS) and *Current Population Survey* (CPS) household typologies to a common format is necessary in order to project future demand for rental housing. A linear projection of historic owner/renter tenure shares (AHS) for each household configuration indicates the following trendlines to 1990:

	1970	1977	1980	1990
Male Head, Wife Present				
Owner	70.7	77.1	79.4	86.9
Renter	29.3	22.9	20.6	13.1
Male Head, Other				
Owner	41.2	38.6	37.6	33.9
Renter	58.8	61.4	62.4	66.1
Female Head, Other				
Owner	47.8	47.2	46.9	46.1
Renter	52.2	52.8	53.1	53.9

2. The CPS projection of future households by type reveals the following patterns:

	1980	1990
Total Households	79,870	96,653
Husband-Wife	48,968	54,731
Male Head, Other	10,270	14,874
Female Head, Other	20,633	27,049

3. The product of both the preceding projection sets is an estimation of future rental demand by household type (numbers in thousands):

Household Configuration	1980	1990	Change: 1980 to 1990 Number Present	
Total Renter	27,451	31,581	4,130	15.0%
Male Head, Wife Present	10,087	7,170	-2,917	-28.9
Male Head, Other	6,408	9,832	3,424	53.4
Female Head, Other	10,956	14,579	3,623	33.1
Total Owner	52,420	65,073	12,653	24.1
Total Households	79,871	96,654	16,783	21.0

Thus, 4.1-million additional households will be seeking rental accommodations over the decade of the 1980s, despite a substantial shrinkage of "male head, wife present" households in the rental demand equation.

4. Concurrently, 12.6-million households are projected to require ownership tenure, resulting in an overall growth in households approaching 16.8 million.

5. This pattern of anticipated demand reflects the general maintenance of trends evidenced during the 1970s:

	Change: 1970 to 1977	Average Annual Change
Renter Households	2,954	422
Owner Households	8,880	1,269

	Change: 1980 to 1990	Average Annual Change
Renter Households	4,130	413
Owner Households	12,653	1,265

In annualized terms the growth in owner and renter households is consistent for the two time periods. Thus, the major area of expansion, economic and financial conditions permitting, will continue to be in ownership tenure.

3

Housing Supply:
Changing Inventory Parameters

The supply side of America's housing markets is at one and the same time the result of increases in household formations, shifts in configurations and arrangements, and changes in fiscal competence and desire to utilize alternative shelter formats. As comprehensive as this list may be, the relationship—or directions of causality—also can be reversed. The supply sector strongly shapes the structure of housing demand.

Rather than merely being passive and/or dependent, it is the supply of housing of various formats (physical and tenurial) within given price sectors that may vitally affect household formations and configurations—the capacity, for example, of households to undouble in periods of affluence, or conversely, in periods of higher costs and restricted shelter availability, to redouble.

Thus, supply is both a reflection and an instigator of demand functions. While this chapter on supply is analytically partitioned from the demand analysis of the preceding chapter, it should be kept in mind that they are inextricably linked.

Changes in the Housing Inventory: 1960 to 1978

Despite the ominous forebodings of impending supply shortfalls over the last generation by a variety of presidential commissions, America's housing inventory has been able to provide the accommodations that made feasible the household growth documented above. From 1960 to 1970, slightly more than 10-million housing units were added to the nation's inventory, an increment comparable in magnitude to that achieved in any previous intercensal decade (Exhibit 1). But, in the first eight years of the 1970s alone, this total was surpassed by more than 50 percent. With almost 1.75-million housing starts recorded in 1979 (Exhibit 2), the 1970s were the most prolific housing decade in the nation's annals.

By 1978, America's shelter supply had reached truly awesome proportions: 84.6-million total units. And what makes this achievement even more remarkable was that this figure was achieved despite the concurrent rapid residential abandonment that afflicted the housing inventories of the nation's aging urban centers (See Appendix A).

Thus, despite very substantial inventory deletions—the nation's annual overall scrappage rate in the past decade averaged nearly 1 percent of the total supply—the decade ended with America's housing stock expanding by over 17-million units. Not only were unsurpassed gains in single-family units recorded, but also record quantities of rental facilities. The 3.3-million net rental additions secured over the 1970 to 1978 period were within 9,000 units of the total achieved in the entire preceding decade (Exhibit 1).

But, the 1970s will be primarily remembered as an era of homeownership aspirations and fulfillment. In the 1975 to 1978 period, for example, almost 5-million single-family unit starts were initiated, over 72 percent of all housing starts (Exhibit 2). While one-unit structures cannot be completely synonymized with homeownership (the largest single segment of our rental housing stock comprises single-unit structures), the long-term shift by Americans into this preferred form of tenure is shown in Exhibit 3. As late as 1940, the United States was primarily a nation of renters. The cessation of World War II and the prior Depression brought with it a tremendous growth of homeownership. By 1978, 65.2 percent of the nation's households were homeowners (with more recent data not shown here indicating the ownership rate now exceeding the two-thirds mark). And, this has been a phenomenon that has not been inhibited by racial partitions. While the level of ownership of blacks and others still lags behind that of whites, it has been growing at a comparable rate. By 1977, more than four in ten of America's minority group households were owner occupants.

Location

The pattern of location, particularly of rental units, changed quite markedly in the period of the 1970s for which data is available. As shown in Exhibit 4, the major gains were registered in the

EXHIBIT 1

Changes in the Housing Inventory: 1960 to 1978
(numbers in thousands)

	1960	1970	1978	Change: 1960 to 1970		Change: 1970 to 1978	
				Number	Percent	Number	Percent
All Housing Units	58,326	68,672	84,618	10,346	17.7	15,946	23.2
All Year Round Units	56,584	67,699	82,833	11,115	19.6	15,134	22.4
Occupied Units	53,024	63,445	77,167	10,421	19.7	13,722	21.6
Owner Occupied	32,797	39,886	50,283	7,089	21.6	10,397	26.1
Percent of Total	61.9	62.9	65.2	—		—	
Renter Occupied	20,227	23,560	26,884	3,333	16.5	3,324	14.1
Percent of Total	38.1	37.1	34.8	—		—	

Source: U.S. Bureau of the Census. *Census of Population and Housing: 1960 and 1970;* and *Current Housing Reports,* Series H-150-78, Annual Housing Survey: 1978, part A. *General Characteristics for the United States and Regions.* Washington, D.C.: U.S. Government Printing Office, 1980.

EXHIBIT 2

New Privately Owned Housing Units Started, by Structure Size, United States Total: 1964 to 1979
(numbers in thousands)

					IN STRUCTURES WITH—			
	Total		*1 Unit*		*2 to 4 Units*		*5 Units or More*	
Year	*Number*	*Percent*	*Number*	*Percent*	*Number*	*Percent*	*Number*	*Percent*
1964	1,529	100.0	971	63.5	108	7.1	450	29.4
1965	1,473	100.0	964	65.4	87	5.9	422	28.6
1966	1,165	100.0	779	66.9	61	5.2	325	27.9
1967	1,292	100.0	844	65.3	72	5.6	376	29.1
1968	1,508	100.0	899	59.6	82	5.4	527	34.9
1969	1,467	100.0	811	55.3	85	5.8	571	38.9
1970	1,434	100.0	813	56.7	85	5.9	536	37.4
1971	2,052	100.0	1,151	56.1	120	5.8	781	38.1
1972	2,356	100.0	1,309	55.6	141	6.0	906	38.5
1973	2,045	100.0	1,132	55.4	118	5.8	795	38.9
1974	1,338	100.0	888	66.4	68	5.1	382	28.6
1975	1,160	100.0	892	76.9	64	5.5	204	17.6
1976	1,538	100.0	1,162	75.5	87	5.7	289	18.8
1977	1,987	100.0	1,451	73.0	122	6.1	414	20.8
1978	2,020	100.0	1,433	70.9	125	6.2	462	22.9
1979	1,745	100.0	1,194	68.4	122	7.0	429	24.6
Total 1964 to 1979	26,109	100.0	16,693	63.9	1,547	5.9	7,869	30.1

Note: Percents may not add due to rounding.

Source: U.S. Bureau of the Census, Department of Commerce, *Construction Reports*, "Housing Starts," C20-78-10. Washington, D.C.: U.S. Government Printing Office, December 1978; also, C20-80-7, September 1980.

suburban areas (not in central cities) of SMSAs. This trend was most marked in the rental housing sector. Central cities secured a net addition only slightly in excess of 700,000 rental units—the nation as a whole had a comparable increase of over 3.3-million rental units. By 1978, central cities accounted for 43.9 percent of the rental housing units of the country, as compared to 56.1 percent for suburban and nonmetropolitan (outside SMSAs) areas.

EXHIBIT 3

Occupied Housing Units—Tenure by Race of Household Head:
1920 to 1978

(Prior to 1960, excludes Alaska and Hawaii.
Tenure allocated for housing units that did not report.)

Year, Race, and Residence	Total	OCCUPIED UNITS [1] (Numbers in Thousands)				Average Annual Percent Change [2]
		Owner Occupied		Renter Occupied		Total Occupied Units
		Number	Percent	Number	Percent	
TOTAL						
1920	24,352	11,114	45.6	13,238	54.4	1.9
1930	29,905	14,280	47.8	15,624	52.2	2.1
1940	34,855	15,196	43.6	19,659	56.4	1.5
1950	42,826	23,560	55.0	19,266	45.0	2.1
1960	53,024	32,797	61.9	20,227	38.1	2.2
1970	63,445	39,886	62.9	23,560	37.1	1.8
1976	74,005	47,904	64.7	26,101	35.3	2.0
1977	75,280	48,765	64.8	26,515	35.2	1.7
1978	77,167	50,283	65.2	26,884	34.8	2.5
RACE						
White:						
1920	21,826	10,511	48.2	11,315	51.8	(NA)
1930	26,983	13,544	50.2	13,439	49.8	2.1
1940	31,561	14,418	45.7	17,143	54.3	1.6
1950	39,044	22,241	57.0	16,803	43.0	2.2
1960	47,880	30,823	64.4	17,057	35.6	2.1
1970	56,529	36,979	65.4	19,551	34.6	1.7
1976	65,114	44,024	67.6	21,090	32.4	2.0
1977	66,111	44,762	67.7	21,349	32.3	1.5
Black and Other:						
1920	2,526	603	23.9	1,923	76.1	(NA)
1930	2,922	737	25.2	2,185	74.8	1.5
1940	3,293	778	23.6	2,516	76.4	1.2
1950	3,783	1,319	34.9	2,464	65.1	1.4
1960	5,144	1,974	38.4	3,171	61.6	3.1
1970	6,920	2,907	42.0	4,014	58.0	3.0
1976	8,891	3,880	43.6	5,011	56.4	2.6
1977	9,169	4,003	43.7	5,165	56.3	3.1

(Notes continued on next page)

Notes: 1. Statistics on the number of occupied units are essentially comparable although identified by various terms—the term "family" applies to figures for 1910 and 1930; "occupied dwelling unit," 1940 and 1950; and "occupied housing unit," 1960, 1970, 1975, and 1976. For 1920, includes the small number of quasi-families; for 1930 represents private families only.

2. For 1920, change from 1910.

Source: U.S. Bureau of the Census, *Census of Population and Housing; 1960 and 1970;* and *Current Housing Reports,* Series H-150-78, Annual Housing Survey: 1978, Part A. *General Characteristics for the United States and Regions.* Washington, D.C.: U.S. Government Printing Office, 1980.

Changes in the Inventory of Rental Housing

Structure Type

What kinds of structures are embodied within the overall universe of renter occupied units? In Exhibit 5, the basic parameters in this regard are isolated for 1970 and 1978. Even though declining, a major configuration comprises one-family homes (1-unit detached), with more than 7-million renter occupied units so classified as of 1978. An even more significant sector, one with the largest single absolute growth increment, comprises two- to four-unit structures, which incorporated more than 7.4-million renter occupied units in 1978.

Relatively large scale structures represent a distinct minority within the total inventory, with less than 2.5-million rental units in structures containing 50 or more units as of 1978. It is striking to note that in the period under consideration, the fastest rate of growth was evidenced by mobile homes or trailers, which almost doubled.

Thus, the supply of rental housing is far more heterogeneous than is sometimes understood. While the conventional vision, particularly in major cities in the Northeast, is one of large scale structures and complexes, this certainly is not borne out by national profiles. Thus, the issues of securing some uniformity of maintenance, of service delivery, and of promulgating expertise are magnified by the sheer variety of structures that are involved.

Age

These latter difficulties are further compounded by the great age spectrum that exists within the inventory. Over 40 percent of it is more than forty years old (10.9-million out of 26.9-million units). As of 1978, barely 17 percent of it (4.6-million units) had been built within the 1970s. As noted in more substantial detail in

EXHIBIT 4

Occupied Housing Units—Tenure by SMSA Status: 1970 and 1978
(numbers in thousands)

| | Total | INSIDE SMSAs | | | Outside SMSAs |
		Total	In Central Cities	Not in Central Cities	
Occupied Units					
1970: Number	63,445	43,859	21,395	22,464	19,586
Percent	100.0	69.1	33.7	35.4	30.9
1978: Number	77,167	52,722	23,436	29,286	24,444
Percent	100.0	68.3	30.4	38.0	31.7
Owner Occupied					
1970: Number	39,886	26,090	10,300	15,790	13,796
Percent	100.0	65.4	25.8	39.6	34.6
1978: Number	50,283	32,390	11,630	20,760	17,892
Percent	100.0	64.4	23.1	41.3	35.6
Renter Occupied					
1970: Number	23,560	17,769	11,095	6,674	5,790
Percent	100.0	75.4	47.1	28.3	24.6
1978: Number	26,884	20,332	11,806	8,526	6,552
Percent	100.0	75.6	43.9	31.7	24.4

Note: Numbers and/or percents may not add due to rounding.

Source: U.S. Department of Commerce, U.S. Bureau of the Census. *Current Housing Reports*, Series H-150-78; *General Housing Characteristics for the United States and Regions: 1978*, Annual Housing Survey: 1978, Part A. Washington, D.C.: U.S. Government Printing Office, 1980.

Appendix A, there were significant deletions from the inventory in the course of eight years. Typically, these were concentrated at the older end of the age spectrum, with more than one in five (20.6 percent) of all units built in the 1940s having disappeared from the rental inventory by the terminal year of Exhibit 5. (Some of this may well have been temporary Veterans Housing built during World War II.) Based on recent HUD studies of condominium conversion, there does not seem to be a probability that the latter process impacted rental deletions to any great measure in the years prior to 1978 (See Appendix B).

Rooms Per Unit

The actual scale of individual rental units is much more consistent than the structural configuration in which they are incorporated. As shown in Exhibit 5, there is a basic clustering at the three- to five-rooms-per-unit level. Over the period of 1970 to 1978, the greatest level of growth was in three- (20.5 percent, and four- (22.1 percent) room units.

Facilities

As the other characteristics of the inventory are examined, i.e., complete kitchen facilities, plumbing, and complete bathrooms, it is evident that significant levels of upgrading have taken place (at least as measured by the very presence of these facilities). Barely 3 percent of America's occupied rental facilities lack complete kitchen facilities, and similarly low proportions lacked plumbing facilities or complete bathrooms (Exhibit 5). While not minimizing the possibilities of families in distress suffering from a lack of basic amenities, the improvements do indicate the relatively small scale of such lagging elements within the rental housing stock.

Gross Rent

Within this context of increased amenities, there is the issue of changing rent levels. And, here the trendlines are much less sanguine (Exhibit 5). There was a two-thirds (69.6 percent) shrinkage in the number of units renting for less than $100 in the eight-year period encompassed by the data. More than one in three (43.7 percent) of the units renting between $100 to $149 had either been physically removed from the inventory (see Appendix A) or had escalated to higher rent levels. At the other end of the rent spectrum, rapid growth increments were recorded in the $200 to $299 (654.2 percent) and $300 or more (1,221.9 percent) sectors.

EXHIBIT 5

Renter Occupied Units
Inventory Characteristics
(numbers in thousands)

	1970	1978	Change: 1970 to 1978 Number	Percent
Units in Structure				
TOTAL	23,560	26,884	3,324	14.1%
1, Detached	7,736	7,196	−540	−7.0
1, Attached	794	1,101	307	38.7
2 to 4	6,218	7,426	1,208	19.4
5 to 19	4,503	5,992	1,489	33.1
20 to 49	1,873	2,039	166	8.9
50 or more	2,115	2,491	376	17.8
Mobile Home or Trailer	321	639	318	99.1
Year Structure Built				
TOTAL	23,560	26,884	3,324	14.1%
April 1970 or later	−	4,616	4,616	−
1965 to March 1970	2,813	3,137	324	11.5
1960 to 1964	2,476	2,369	−107	−4.3
1950 to 1959	3,647	3,259	−388	−10.6
1940 to 1949	3,264	2,591	−673	−20.6
1939 or Earlier	11,361	10,910	−451	−4.0
Rooms Per Unit				
TOTAL	23,560	26,884	3,324	14.1%
1 room	944	1,034	90	9.5
2 rooms	1,763	1,773	10	0.6
3 rooms	5,381	6,486	1,105	20.5
4 rooms	7,088	8,655	1,567	22.1
5 rooms	4,705	5,088	383	8.1
6 rooms	2,385	2,473	88	3.7
7 rooms or more	1,294	1,376	82	6.3
Median	4.0	4.0	0	0.0
Complete Kitchen Facilities				
TOTAL	23,560	26,884	3,324	14.1%
For Exclusive use of Household	22,327	25,945	3,618	16.2
Not for Exclusive use of Household	1,232	939	−293	−23.8
Plumbing Facilities				
TOTAL	23,560	26,884	3,324	14.1%
With All	21,711	25,811	4,100	18.9
Lacking Some or All	1,849	1,073	−776	−42.0

EXHIBIT 5 (Continued)

	1970	1978	Change: 1970 to 1978	
			Number	Percent
Complete Bathrooms				
TOTAL	23,560	26,884	3,324	14.1%
Complete	21,384	25,641	4,257	19.9
None or Share	2,176	1,243	−933	−42.9
Gross Rent				
TOTAL (Specified Renter Occupied)	22,334	26,246	3,912	17.5%
Less than $100	9,167	2,789	−6,378	−69.6
$100 to $149	7,104	3,999	−3,105	−43.7
$150 to $199	3,304	5,666	2,362	71.5
$200 to $299	1,194	9,005	7,811	654.2
$300 or more	265	3,503	3,238	1,221.9
No cash rent	1,300	1,285	—	—
Median	$108	$200	$92	85.2%

Source: U.S. Department of Commerce, U.S. Bureau of the Census. *Current Housing Reports*, Series H-150-78; *General Housing Characteristics for the United States and Regions: 1978*, Annual Housing Survey: 1978, Part A. Washington, D.C.: U.S. Government Printing Office, 1980.

In the interpretation of the magnitude of the shifts in rent distributions, it must be stressed that the two pools of housing (that of 1970 versus that of 1978) are quite distinct. The data reflect not only rent adjustments to long-standing rental units, but also inventory deletions (predominantly low rent) and new construction (principally high rent). Nonetheless, from the renter aspirant perspective, the bottom line was literally a shift in median rents required from $108 to $200.

Regional Shifts

In general, new rental housing facilities were added in consonance with the population shifts that had taken place in the United States. As shown in Exhibit 6, for example, the slowest growth, both in ownership and in rental units, was in the Northeast, with rates of increase at the 11.2- and 9.9-percent levels, respectively. The North Central Region, on the other hand, enjoyed absolute increments half again as large in each of the sectors. Both the South and the West, conversely, showed larger growth rates of owner occupancy compared to rental accommodations. In both cases, however, their magnitude of rental gains was double that of the Northeast. Thus, only one out of ten- rental units in the Northeast was built post-1970 (using 1978 as a terminal year). In the South the equivalent

EXHIBIT 6

Units Constructed 1970 to 1978, Percent of 1978 Total,
by Tenure and Region
(numbers in thousands)

	Total 1978	New Construction 1970 to 1978	New Construction Percent of 1978 Total
U.S. Total			
Occupied (Total)	77,167	15,192	19.7%
Owner Occupied	50,283	10,576	21.0
Renter Occupied	26,884	4,616	17.2
Northeast			
Occupied (Total)	16,952	1,814	10.7
Owner Occupied	10,155	1,142	11.2
Renter Occupied	6,797	673	9.9
North Central			
Occupied (Total)	20,171	3,331	16.5
Owner Occupied	14,152	2,369	16.7
Renter Occupied	6,019	962	16.0
South			
Occupied (Total)	25,094	6,423	25.6
Owner Occupied	16,885	4,612	27.3
Renter Occupied	8,208	1,811	22.1
West			
Occupied (Total)	14,950	3,624	24.2
Owner Occupied	9,091	2,453	27.0
Renter Occupied	5,859	1,171	20.0

Note: Numbers and/or percents may not add due to rounding.

Source: U.S. Department of Commerce, U.S. Bureau of the Census. *Current Housing Reports*, Series H-150-78; *General Housing Characteristics for the United States and Regions: 1978*, Annual Housing Survey: 1978, Part A. Washington, D.C.: U.S. Government Printing Office, 1980.

parameter would be more than one in five, with the West also approaching that level. To the degree that housing maintenance problems are linked with the geriatric diseases caused by age, it is the Northeast that will suffer most substantially. Conversely, it is the growth areas of the country that will have the greatest level of flexibility—of a relatively new rental inventory—with which to enhance the capacity to secure newcomers.

Summary

1. From 1970 to 1978, over 13-million year round housing units were added to the nation's housing inventory, an increment far greater than the 11-million net additions recorded over the *entire* 1960 to 1970 decade.

2. While the 1970 to 1978 gains of the renter occupied sector (3.3-million units) were less than one-third of those registered by owner occupied units (10.4-million units), their absolute magnitude matched that of the entire preceding decade (3.3-million units). It is highly probable that the net rental gains of the 1970s will exceed that of any preceding intercensal decade, at least since 1920.

3. Thus, rental housing's declining share of the total inventory is not due to the lack of growth in this sector. It is the result of unparalleled expansion in homeownership during a decade that has been the most prolific housing period in America's history.

4. Indeed, the 1970s recorded an acceleration of long-term trends toward homeownership. As late as 1940, renter occupied units accounted for 56.4 percent of the total occupied housing stock. By 1978, the rental share declined to 34.8 percent. This long-term shift has been marked across all geographic partitions and racial groups.

5. The expansion of the rental sector has taken place principally in the suburban areas of SMSAs and in nonmetropolitan areas. By 1978, central cities accounted for only 43.9 percent of all renter occupied units. On a regional base, the South and West secured the largest shares of new construction, the Northeast the smallest share. Within the latter region, only one out of ten (9.9 percent) renter occupied units was built from 1970 to 1978. In the South and West, the corresponding share was one out of five (22.1 and 20.0 percent, respectively).

6. As of 1978, the bulk of the nation's rental units (26.9-million total units) were located in 2- to 4-unit structures (7.4-million units) and one-family detached structures (7.2-million units). Only 2.5-million units were located in buildings containing 50 or more units. Thus, the supply of rental housing is far more heterogeneous than is sometimes understood.

7. At the same time, the actual scale of individual rental units is much more consistent than the structural configuration in which they are incorporated. The vast majority of rental units contain three to five rooms, with the median (4.0 rooms) remaining constant over the 1970 to 1978 period.

8. The 1970s also witnessed the increasing presence of full amenities in the rental inventory, at least as measured by complete kitchens, bathrooms, and full plumbing facilities.

9. Concurrently, however, the median monthly gross rent increased from $108 in 1970 to $200 by 1978, an 80.5 percent increase. The number of units renting for under $150 contracted sharply, while over 11.5-million units surged above the $200 per-month threshold.

4

The Changing Rental Market: Demand and Supply Interrelationships

---

It is the market arena wherein the population of households is matched to the housing stock. The functioning of the rental market— its effective allocation of shelter to those requiring or demanding it—is revealed by a select set of indicators detailing the intersection of demand and supply variables. Such extant "pulse takers" of the market, however, are limited in number, nor are they entirely comprehensive in terms of coverage. Nonetheless, they are probably sufficient to reveal at least the broader contours of the rental market landscape.

In this chapter, three major variables will be examined. Rent-income ratios, first to be considered, relate the cost of consuming rental housing to income availability. Changes in rent-income ratios reveal the relative shifts in the income/cost relationships, i.e., the "fit" of housing expenditures within the context of income resources. Persons per room (a measure of internal housing density, or overcrowding) measures the "fit" of a household to its housing accommodations, i.e., an index gauging the allocation of the quantity of physical space to individual households. The final indicator is the vacancy rate, changes in which gauge the relative rates of change in the supply of housing versus the demand for it. The evolution of these indices over the decade of the 1970s reveals significant shifts within the rental housing market.

EXHIBIT 1

Median Family Income and Consumer Price Index, United States: 1950 to 1979

Year	Median Family Income		Consumer Price Index All Items
	Actual Dollars	Constant 1979 Dollars	
1950	$ 3,319	$10,008	72.1
1955	4,418	11,979	80.2
1960	5,620	13,774	88.7
1965	6,957	16,005	94.5
1970	9,867	18,444	116.3
1975	13,719	18,502	161.2
1977	16,009	19,176	181.5
1978	17,640	19,626	195.4
1979	19,684	19,684	217.7

Gains in Real Income
(Constant 1979 Dollars)

Period			
1950 to 1960	←	$3,766 ←	37.6%
1950 to 1955		1,971	19.7
1955 to 1960		1,795	15.0
1960 to 1970	←	4,670 ←	33.9
1960 to 1965		2,231	16.2
1965 to 1970		2,439	15.2
1970 to 1979	←	1,240 ←	6.7
1970 to 1975		58	0.3
1975 to 1979		1,182	6.4

Source: U.S. Bureau of the Census. Current Population Reports, Series P-60, no. 125, *Money Income and Poverty Status of Families and Persons in the United States: 1979* (Advance Report). Washington, D.C.: U.S. Government Printing Office, 1980.

Before fully directing our attention to these matters, it is useful to first examine longer-term income and inflationary dynamics in order to provide an appropriate analytical context. While renter income "shortfalls" have already been documented in chapter one, a longer-term perspective provides even more emphasis to the depth of the problem.

Income and Inflationary Dynamics

The housing buying power of all Americans has been impacted by the slow growth in real incomes, and relatively fast growth in the cost of shelter. This latter element has been most accentuated in the field of homeownership where occupancy costs have exceeded the Consumer Price Index (CPI). But, even in the field of rental housing, where rent increases have until very recently lagged behind the CPI, the same phenomenon holds true, but in this case it is exacerbated by the degeneration in relative income capacities discussed earlier.

Income Stabilization

Exhibit 2 provides some of the key elements that detail the relationships between median family income and the CPI from 1950 to 1979. The period was initiated by a vigorous increase in *real* incomes, as indicated in the lower portions of the exhibit. From 1950 to 1960, real incomes (in constant 1979 dollars) increased by 37.6 percent or $3,766. The decade of the 1960s witnessed an even higher absolute gain ($4,670), but at a somewhat lower rate (33.9 percent). Nonetheless, for every three dollars earned in 1960, the median family had four of equivalent buying power a decade later.

The pattern evidenced in the 1970s, however, indicates an abrupt decline in long-term-real-income gains. Stabilization characterized the 1970 to 1975 period, followed by a modest gain in the 1975 to 1979 period of 6.4 percent ($1,182). (It should be noted further that data not shown here indicates that even this latter increment had suffered some degree of attrition through 1980.) Thus, real median family incomes in the United States, which registered a near doubling between 1950 to 1970, have reached an imperiled stability as the 1980s begin.

Inflationary Dynamics

Impending limits to effective housing buying power are illuminated somewhat by the surging inflationary dynamic that has built up over the past two decades. As shown in the bottom of Exhibit 2, the four successive five-year periods between 1960 and 1980 have reflected the following increases in the CPI: 6.5, 23.1, 38.6, and 53.8 percent, respectively. Clearly, the latter increases have exerted considerable pressures on income capacities. And, any projection based on this historical foundation would portend ominous difficulties for the 1980s.

In addition, within the shifts in the CPI, there were substantial variations in the principal elements that comprise shelter. Rents, as shown in Exhibit 2, have clearly lagged behind the overall "all items" index. As late as July 1980, they had reached a level only 80 percent that of the overal CPI. This occurred despite ferocious increases in energy costs documented in the exhibit.

EXHIBIT 2

Consumer Price Index, United States, Selected Items:
1960 to 1980

Year	All [1] Items	Home Ownership	Rent	Fuel Oil And Coal	Gas and Electricity
1960	88.7	86.3	91.7	89.2	98.6
1965	94.5	92.7	96.9	94.6	99.4
1970	116.3	128.5	110.1	110.1	107.3
1971	121.3	133.7	115.2	117.5	114.7
1972	125.3	140.1	119.2	118.5	120.5
1973	133.1	146.7	124.3	136.0	126.4
1974	147.7	163.2	130.6	214.6	145.8
1975	161.2	181.7	137.3	235.3	169.6
1976	170.5	191.7	144.7	250.8	189.0
1977	181.5	204.9	153.5	283.4	213.4
1978	195.4	227.2	164.0	298.3	232.6
1979	217.7	263.6	175.9	403.6	257.9
1980 (July)	248.0	317.9	191.8	561.9	313.5

Percentage Change

Period					
1960 to 1970	31.1	48.9	20.1	23.4	8.8
1960 to 1965	6.5	7.4	5.7	6.1	0.8
1965 to 1970	23.1	38.6	13.6	16.4	7.9
1970 to 1980	113.2	147.4	74.2	410.4	192.2
1970 to 1975	38.6	41.4	24.7	113.7	58.1
1975 to 1980	53.8	75.0	39.7	138.8	84.8

Note: 1. Overall CPI, Urban Wage Earners, and Clerical Workers.

Source: Bureau of Economic Analysis, U.S. Department of Commerce. *Survey of Current Business.* Washington, D.C.: U.S. Government Printing Office, Annual.

   The situation for homeownership differed substantially, with a virtual tripling of this component from 1970 through mid-1980. Thus, while median incomes barely kept pace with inflation, home-ownership costs soared beyond the overall CPI, while rent levels—though showing signs of decided increase in the last several years for which data are presented—have lagged behind the overall (all items) index.

   However, the CPI rental component differs substantially from that gauged by the Annual Housing Survey (see Exhibit 6, chapter three), with the latter indicating considerably higher rent increments. This discrepancy is the result of the CPI attempting to establish the changing prices of standardized goods and services over time. What is being measured is the changing price of a rental unit of consistent amenity and quality over a period of years. However, the modular dwelling unit employed by the CPI may be a decreasingly significant part of the rental inventory over the course of time, since additions (at higher rents) and deletions (typically lower rents) are constantly altering the rental housing reservoir. It is the Annual Housing Survey that provides the best measure of the overall rent structures that confront the overall pool of renter aspirants over time.

Rent-Income Ratios

The interaction of the cost-income factors—rent-income ratios— is illustrated in the series of exhibits that follow. The first, Exhibit 3, provides an overview for all renter occupied units from 1970 to 1978. The overall median ratio increased from 20 percent of income to 25 percent in the brief eight-year period. Thus, the threshold level of much in the way of federal and state housing aid legislation, i.e., that individuals should not pay more than 25 percent of their incomes for rent, clearly was violated by fully half of all renters in the United States as of 1978. While definitive data on more recent relationships are not yet available, it is evident that if anything this ratio has degenerated in the interim. By 1978, nearly three in ten of all renters were paying 35 percent or more of their incomes for rent. The absolute number of renters under the 15-percent mark had declined by nearly a third.

The same relationships are evident when the data are partitioned by household configurations for 1973 and 1978 (see Exhibits 4 and 5). Note first that there is a relatively small variation in median gross rents across the profile of household types. The range in 1973, for example, is a relatively modest one, spanning from $1,344 annually for "other male headed" households sixty-five-years of age and over to a peak of $1,860 for young "male head, wife present" households. When this variation is contrasted with the much greater spectrum of median income levels, the result is the wide disparity in the proportion of incomes that must be devoted to rent.

The same process is evident, and even more accentuated, when these data are compared to their 1978 equivalents. By the latter year, while "male head, wife present" households still had relatively modest rent-income ratios (19.4 percent), the ratio for female headed households had soared above the 35-percent level (35.8 percent). The only improvements in this vital expenditure element were a relatively minor shift from 30.7 to 30.3 percent registered by one-person households, reflecting the more youthful, higher

EXHIBIT 3

Gross Rent as a Percent of Income: Total Renter Occupied
Units—1970 to 1978
(numbers in thousands)

	1970	1978	Change: 1970 to 1978 Number	Percent
Specified Renter Occupied	22,334	26,246	3,912	17.5%
Less than 10 percent	2,012	1,337	−675	−33.5
10 to 14 percent	3,979	3,277	−702	−17.6
15 to 19 percent	3,786	4,081	295	7.8
20 to 24 percent	2,657	3,819	1,162	43.7
25 to 34 percent	2,936	4,695	1,759	59.9
35 percent or more	5,209	7,622	2,413	46.3
Not computed	1,756	1,415	−	−
Median	20%	25%	5%	25.0

Source: U.S. Department of Commerce, U.S. Bureau of the Census. *Current Housing Reports*, Series H-150-78, *General Housing Characteristics for the United States and Regions: 1978*, Annual Housing Survey: 1978, Part A. Washington, D.C.: U.S. Government Printing Office, 1980.

incomed, newcomers to that part of the market, and somewhat more substantial improvements evidenced by the elderly, resulting from income gains accruing from inflationary indexed social security payments.

Gross Rent-Income Ratios for Central City Black Households

In 1973, all "two-or-more person" black renter households had a rent-income ratio well under the 25-percent threshold: 21.8 percent (Exhibit 6). By 1978, the ratio had risen to 27.5 percent (Exhibit 7). Practically all of this increment related to households other than husband-wife configurations. Female headed households experienced the greatest impact, shifting from allocating 24.9 to 34.1 percent of their total income dollars for rents. While for all U.S. one-person renter households there had been some minor alleviation of rent-income ratios, among blacks there was more substantial improvement: from 31.9 percent of income required for rents in 1973 to a still onerous 30.6 percent by 1978.

EXHIBIT 4

Median Rent as a Percent of Median Income: U.S. Total, 1973

Household Composition by Age of Head	1973 Median Income	1973 Monthly Median Gross Rent	1973 Annual Median Gross Rent	1973 Median Rent as a Percent of Median Income
2-or-More Person Households	$ 8,600	$141	$1,692	19.6
Male Head, Wife Present	9,500	144	1,728	18.2
Under 25 Years	8,300	137	1,644	19.8
25 to 29 Years	10,700	155	1,860	17.4
30 to 34 Years	10,900	154	1,848	17.0
35 to 44 Years	10,800	154	1,848	17.1
45 to 64 Years	10,400	142	1,704	16.4
65 Years and Over	4,900	121	1,452	29.6
Other Male Head	8,600	151	1,812	21.0
Under 65 Years	9,000	155	1,860	20.7
65 Years and Over	4,800	112	1,344	28.0
Female Head	5,800	130	1,560	26.9
Under 65 Years	5,900	131	1,572	26.6
65 Years and Over	4,600	119	1,428	31.0
1-Person Households	4,500	115	1,380	30.7

Source: U.S. Department of Commerce, U.S. Bureau of the Census. *Current Housing Report*, Series H-150-78, *General Housing Characteristics for the United States and Regions: 1978,* Annual Housing Survey: 1978, Part A. Washington, D.C.: U.S. Government Printing Office, 1980.

EXHIBIT 5

Median Rent as a Percent of Income: U.S. Total, 1978

Household Composition by Age of Head	1978 Median Income	1978 Monthly Median Gross Rent	1978 Annual Median Gross Rent	1978 Median Rent as a Percent of Median Income
2-or-More Person Households	$10,900	$216	$2,592	23.8%
Male Head, Wife Present	13,700	221	2,652	19.4
Under 25 Years	11,900	209	2,508	21.1
25 to 29 Years	14,400	224	2,688	18.7
30 to 34 Years	15,900	234	2,808	17.7
35 to 44 Years	16,000	237	2,844	17.8
45 to 64 Years	14,400	222	2,664	18.5
65 Years and Over	8,100	196	2,352	29.0
Other Male Head	10,200	236	2,832	27.8
Under 65 Years	10,400	238	2,856	27.5
65 Years and Over	8,100	168	2,016	24.9
Female Head	6,600	197	2,364	35.8
Under 65 Years	6,600	199	2,388	36.2
65 Years and Over	6,600	161	1,932	29.3
1-Person Households	6,900	174	2,088	30.3

Source: U.S. Department of Commerce, U.S. Bureau of the Census. *Current Housing Report*, Series H-150-78, *General Housing Characteristics for the United States and Regions: 1978*, Annual Housing Survey: 1978, Part A. Washington, D.C.: U.S. Government Printing Office, 1980.

EXHIBIT 6

Median Rent as a Percent of Income: Central City Black Households, 1973

Household Composition by Age of Head	1973 Median Income	1973 Monthly Median Gross Rent	1973 Annual Median Gross Rent	1973 Median Rent as a Percent of Median Income
2-or-More Person Households	$ 6,500	$118	$1,416	21.8%
Male Head, Wife Present				
Under 25 Years	8,400	127	1,524	18.1
25 to 29 Years	8,700	120	1,440	16.6
30 to 34 Years	9,700	133	1,596	16.5
35 to 44 Years	10,600	146	1,752	16.5
45 to 64 Years	8,400	133	1,596	19.0
65 Years and Over	6,800	119	1,428	21.0
	3,100	97	1,164	37.5
Other Male Head				
Under 65 Years	5,900	119	1,428	24.2
65 Years and Over	6,300	125	1,500	23.8
	—	—	—	—
Female Head				
Under 65 Years	5,300	110	1,320	24.9
65 Years and Over	5,400	109	1,308	24.2
	4,400	120	1,440	32.7
1-Person Households	3,500	93	1,116	31.9

Note: Numbers and/or percents may not add due to rounding.

Source: U.S. Department of Commerce, U.S. Bureau of the Census. *Current Housing Reports*, Series H-150-73, *General Housing Characteristics for the United States and Regions: 1973*, Annual Housing Survey: 1973, Part A. Washington, D.C.: U.S. Government Printing Office, 1980.

EXHIBIT 7

Median Rent as a Percent of Income: Central City Black Households, 1978

Household Composition by Age of Head	1978 Median Income	1978 Monthly Median Gross Rent	1978 Annual Median Gross Rent	1978 Median Rent as a Percent of Median Income
2-or-More Person Households	$ 7,500	$172	$2,064	27.5%
Male Head, Wife Present				
Under 25 Years	12,300	187	2,244	18.2
25 to 29 Years	11,000	177	2,124	19.3
30 to 34 Years	13,300	194	2,328	17.5
35 to 44 Years	13,500	197	2,364	17.5
45 to 64 Years	14,700	205	2,460	16.7
65 Years and Over	12,200	177	2,124	17.4
	6,000	154	1,848	30.8
Other Male Head				
Under 65 Years	9,300	184	2,208	23.7
65 Years and Over	9,800	184	2,208	22.5
	—	—	—	—
Female Head				
Under 65 Years	5,600	159	1,908	34.1
65 Years and Over	5,500	160	1,920	34.9
	7,100	121	1,452	20.5
1-Person Households	5,300	135	1,620	30.6

Note: Numbers and/or percents may not add due to rounding.

Source: U.S. Department of Commerce, U.S. Bureau of the Census. *Current Housing Reports*, Series H-150-78, *General Housing Characteristics for the United States and Regions: 1978*, Annual Housing Survey: 1978, Part A. Washington, D.C.: U.S. Government Printing Office, 1980.

Summary

Exhibit 8 summarizes the median rent-income ratios presented in the preceding exhibits. Clearly, the crises in affordability of rental housing has had broad impacts. Those who are least stressed are male headed households with wife present (husband-wife families). Whether for all U.S. renters, or for black central city renters, their ratios are a comfortable one-fifth of total incomes. Female headed households are the ones who are forced to carry the heaviest burdens, and this holds true both for all U.S. renters and their black central city counterparts alike. By 1978, such households were at rent levels almost half again as high as the standard that has commonly been set as a maximum impost for shelter: 25 percent.

In addition, their straits are closely approached by one-person households, who pay over 30 percent of their total income dollars for shelter. Thus, the imbalance between incomes and rents is most accentuated in just those segments of the market in which rental housing is securing greatest market penetration. Conversely, rental housing has lost market share and desirability among those clusters of households who have adequate resources to devote to incremental rent levels.

Changing Occupancy Characteristics: Overcrowding

The traditional vision of rental housing, particularly among the low incomed, was one of substantial over-occupancy—of multiple persons per room and the like. That this situation has been changing markedly was already recorded in earlier decennial censuses. But, the basic trends of smaller household configurations appear to have accelerated in more recent years as illustrated in Exhibits 9 and 10. The former provides the number of persons in renter occupied units (household size) for 1970 and 1978. The salient end of the growth spectrum has centered on one-person households, which increased in number by over 2.7 million; the second largest increment was registered by two-person households (990,000). This pattern is completely reversed as the focus is shifted to larger household con- figurations. The number of units occupied by seven or more persons, for example, was reduced by 45 percent in a brief seven-year period; units occupied by six-person groups was reduced by 28.6 percent; and those units with five or more persons by 17.4 percent.

In turn, there has been a massive upgrading in the quality of housing at least as gauged by one of the more commonly used criteria—persons per room (Exhibit 10). In 1970, 3.5 percent of all renter occupied housing units had 1.51 persons or more. By 1977,

EXHIBIT 8

Summary: Renter Households, Median Rent as a Percent of Median Income

	Total U.S. Renters		Black Central City Renters	
	1973	1978	1973	1978
2-or-More Persons Households	19.6	23.8	21.8	27.5
Male Head, Wife Present	18.2	19.4	18.1	18.2
Other Male Head	21.0	27.8	24.2	23.7
Female Head	26.9	35.8	24.9	34.1
1-Person Households	30.7	30.3	31.9	30.6

Source: U.S. Department of Commerce, U.S. Bureau of the Census. *Current Housing Reports*, Series H-150-78, *General Housing Characteristics for the United States and Regions: 1978*, Annual Housing Survey: 1978, Part A. Washington, D.C.: U.S. Government Printing Office, 1980.

EXHIBIT 9

Renter Occupied Housing Units, Persons Per Household: 1970 and 1978 (numbers in thousands)

	1970	1978	Change: 1970 to 1978	
			Number	Percent
Total Renter Occupied	23,560	26,515	2,955	12.5%
1 Person	6,389	9,119	2,730	42.7
2 Persons	6,773	7,772	999	14.7
3 Persons	3,923	4,218	295	7.5
4 Persons	2,875	2,822	−53	−1.8
5 Persons	1,643	1,357	−286	−17.4
6 Persons	915	653	−262	−28.6
7 Persons or More	1,043	574	−469	−45.0
Median (Persons)	2.3	2.0	0.3	−13.0

Source: U.S. Department of Commerce, U.S. Bureau of the Census. *Current Housing Reports*, Series H-150-78, *General Housing Characteristics for the United States and Regions: 1978*, Annual Housing Survey: 1978, Part A. Washington, D.C.: U.S. Government Printing Office, 1980.

less than 2 percent of all America's renter occupied housing units had such levels of overcrowding, a rate of decline of 46.0 percent. If a more strenuous test of overcrowding is applied—units with 1.01 persons or more per room—the results are nearly as salubrious. Indeed, by 1977, more than half of America's rental housing units had .50 persons or fewer per room. In sum, therefore, the age old

EXHIBIT 10

Renter Occupied Housing Units,
Persons Per Room: 1970 and 1978
(numbers in thousands)

| | 1970 | 1978 | Change: 1970 to 1978 | |
			Number	Percent
Total Renter Occupied	23,560	26,515	2,955	12.5%
.50 or less	10,599	14,504	3,905	36.8
.51 to 1.00	10,467	10,367	−100	−1.0
1.01 to 1.50	1,714	1,224	−490	−28.6
1.51 or More	780	421	−359	−46.0

Source: U.S. Department of Commerce, U.S. Bureau of the Census. *Current Housing Reports,* Series H-150-78, *General Housing Characteristics for the United States and Regions: 1978,* Annual Housing Survey: 1978, Part A. Washington, D.C.: U.S. Government Printing Office, 1980.

vision of overcrowding, while still leaving a remnant, has largely been overcome.

Vacancy Rates

The final market indicator to be examined is the vacancy rate. While changes in measurement procedures in 1979 undermine the direct comparability of post-1979 rates to those of earlier years, certain patterns are evident. From 1975 to 1979, when the final segments of the baby boom generation were forming households, the vacancy rate declined across all geographic partitions (Exhibit 11). Since 1979, however, increases in the vacancy rate have been evidenced in general. Whether this shift is a consequence of the maturation to adulthood of the leading edge of the baby bust is as yet uncertain. Nonetheless, the post-1979 trend (measured via revised procedures) differs substantially from that of the preceding four years (measured via older procedures).

The major variation from the general trendline occurs in the Northeast, the setting of least new construction (see chapter three) and the nation's oldest housing stock. Indeed, it is the only region in 1980 whose vacancy rate falls below the 5.0-percent threshold (that level conventionally assumed to represent an adequate rental market). To this degree, it is the only region that evidences a rental supply shortfall in 1980. However, the pace of residential abandonment in the Northeast is probably such as to contribute significantly to this situation, thus suggesting a terminal effect of lagging incomes or excessively high rent-income ratios—inventory deletions.

EXHIBIT 11

Rental Housing Vacancy Rates:
1975 to 1980

	1975	1976	1977	1978	1979[1]	1979[2]	1980[3]
Total Rental Units	6.0	5.6	5.2	5.0	5.0	5.3	5.4
Metropolitan Status							
Inside SMSAs	6.1	5.7	5.3	5.2	5.1	5.4	5.5
Outside SMSAs	5.7	5.1	5.2	4.5	4.8	5.1	5.9
Region							
Northeast	4.1	4.7	5.1	4.8	3.9	4.2	3.9
North Central	5.7	5.6	5.1	4.8	4.8	5.2	5.8
South	7.7	6.4	5.7	5.5	6.1	6.2	6.2
West	6.2	5.4	5.0	4.8	5.1	5.4	5.3

Notes: 1. Old Procedure (second quarter data).
2. Revised procedure instituted (second quarter data).
3. Second quarter data.

Source: U.S. Bureau of the Census. *Current Housing Reports,* "Housing Vacancies: Second Quarter 1980." H-111-80-Q2, August 1980.

Summary

1. As a result of lower income households gaining increased penetration in the rental market—in the context of steadily increasing rents—the overall median rent-income ratio shifted from 20 percent in 1970 to 25 percent by 1978.

2. This pattern of deterioration is evident across the basic profile of renter households.

Median Annual Rent as a Percent of Median Annual Income

	Total U.S. Renters		Black Central City Renters	
	1973	1978	1973	1978
2-or-More Person				
Households	19.6	23.8	21.8	27.5
Male Head, Wife Present	18.2	19.4	18.1	18.2
Other Male Head	21.0	27.8	24.2	23.7
Female Head	26.9	35.8	24.9	34.1
1-Person Households	30.7	30.3	31.9	30.6

The household type with the most favorable ratios—male head, wife present—is precisely that format which is being lost to the rental market. Female headed households, as would be expected, exhibit the most ominous ratios. To reiterate, the latter represents a major growth sector in the rental market.

3. The lack of sharp differentiation between total renters and black central city renters in the preceding tabulation is mainly the result of lower rent levels attendant to the central city inventory. As has been documented previously, their income resources fall far below those of their total renter counterparts.

4. While rent-income ratios have experienced substantial deterioration, there has been a marked improvement in the quantity of housing delivered to renter households. Whatever threshold of overcrowding is employed, it is clear that overcrowding is a problem whose time is past.

5. In general, vacancy rates were far lower at the end of the decade of the 1970s than at the beginning, suggesting that rental demand was growing faster than supply. However, the last two years (1979 and 1980) have seen the rate increase, suggesting a reversal of the decade long pattern.

5

The Uncertain Alternative:
Homeownership

In order to provide an additional reference framework for viewing the rental housing market, it is worthwhile to closely examine some of the analogous financial shifts that have taken place in the alternative to rental tenure: homeownership. As was detailed in the initial portions of the preceding chapter, the costs of homeownership have far outstripped gains in income and have exhibited increases in excess of the CPI in general, and the rental component of the CPI in particular. Yet, the actual and desired shift to ownership tenure has experienced little abatement.

Understanding the reasons for this latter dichotomy is essential in terms of forecasting future housing demand. As detailed earlier, homeownership costs are now offset by a collage of interests. These include not only shelter, but preferential tax treatment and most importantly, inflationary hedging. Rent levels, on the other hand, partake of only the first of these offsets—and thus have been significantly limited by market considerations and the cream skimming of potential renters detailed earlier.

Housing Price Baselines

Within this context the very fact that housing prices go up, rather than being a deterrent to housing ownership demand, have tended to accelerate it—so long as the financing wherewithal has been available. Success has bred more success, i.e., increased demand— more demand!

Reflecting the "new" economic reality are the patterns of median sales prices of new one-family homes sold, which are detailed in Exhibit 1. From 1963 to 1970—a period of relative stability in inflation—the median sales price moved up 30 percent. (It should be further noted that these data are not standardized for quality. A very substantial part of the price increment in all probability represents the improvements both in size and amenities that characterized new housing in that period.) In the following ten-year period from 1970 to 1980, the price increment registered 185.9 percent—with a relatively small proportion resulting from improved amenities.

The dynamics within the several regions of the United States varied substantially, unquestionably reflecting the new regional realities that have altered the face of America. In the first period under consideration, the Northeast, which traditionally had the most expensive housing in the nation, showed an increment in median sales price of nearly 50 percent—more than a third higher than that of the North Central region and nearly double that of the South and West. The pattern from 1970 to 1980, however, was markedly different. The Northeast and North Central states, both relatively slow growth areas in terms of regional population shifts, secured the smallest price gains (127.7 percent and 162.2 percent, respectively). It was the South and West that showed the most dramatic increases with a near doubling in the former region and a 221.7-percent increment in the latter. By June of 1980, the West had the most expensive sales prices for new one-family homes sold in the United States; the other three regions were rapidly approaching parity.

The same phenomenon is evidenced when examination is undertaken of the sales prices of existing single-family homes sold by region, with the increases in the West even more accentuated (Exhibit 2).

The stresses of financing housing in America's new high growth regions, and the shifts of capital that have been required to facilitate this process need little elaboration. It should be noted that the increasingly sophisticated development of the secondary mortgage market was essential if growth was to be accommodated—and this was accomplished with extraordinary economy of time and cost. In large part, the very capital shortages that existed in the West, as a function of the enormous levels of demand there, were frequently reflected in higher mortgage rates than existed elsewhere in the country. Despite this situation, housing prices accelerated; once again surging increments in the cost of this prize asset led more and more individuals and households to make great sacrifices in its behalf.

EXHIBIT 1

Median Sales Prices of New One-Family Houses Sold; United States and Regions: 1963 to 1980

Year	States	Northeast	Region North Central	South	West
1963	$18,000	$20,300	$17,900	$16,100	$18,800
1964	18,900	20,300	19,400	16,700	20,400
1965	20,000	21,500	21.600	17,500	21,600
1966	21,400	23,500	23,200	18,200	23,200
1967	22,700	25,400	25,100	19,400	24,100
1968	24,700	27,700	27,400	21,500	25,100
1969	25,600	31,600	27,600	22,800	25,300
1970	23,400	30,300	24,400	20,300	24,000
1971	25,200	30,600	27,200	22,500	25,500
1972	27,600	31,400	29,300	25,800	27,500
1973	32,500	37,100	32,900	30,900	32,400
1974	35,900	40,100	36,100	34,500	35,800
1975	39,300	44,000	39,600	37,300	40,600
1976	44,200	47,300	44,800	40,500	47,200
1977	48,800	51,600	51,500	44,100	53,500
1978	55,700	58,100	59,200	50,300	61,300
1979	62,900	65,500	63,900	57,300	69,600
1980 (June)[1]	66,900	69,000	63,500	59,400	77,200
Percent Change					
1963 to 1970	30.0%	49.3%	36.3%	26.1%	27.7%
1970 to 1980	185.9	127.7	160.2	192.6	221.7

Note: 1. Preliminary

Source: U.S. Department of Commerce, Bureau of the Census. *Construction Reports*, "New One-Family Houses Sold and For Sale," Series C25-78-10. Washington, D.C.: U.S. Government Printing Office, December 1978. Also: Series C25-71-9, November 1971; C25-78-12, February 1978, and C25-80-7, September 1980.

Income-House Value Relationships

Turning once again to the nation as a whole, the relationship between the median sales price of new one-family houses sold and median family income for the United States from 1954 to 1979 is shown in Exhibit 3. While issue can be raised as to what partitioning of income should be used, i.e., disposable or some other format, the data do provide proximate insights into the relationships that have prevailed. From 1954 through 1968, the ratio of sales price to income hovered close to the 2.9 level. As a function of accelerated government incentive programs (such as Section 235) the ratio

EXHIBIT 2

Median Sales Prices of Existing Single-Family Homes Sold, United States and Regions: 1970 to 1980

Year	States	Northeast	Region North Central	South	West
1970	$23,000	$25,200	$20,100	$22,200	$24,300
1971	24,800	27,100	22,100	24,300	26,500
1972	26,700	29,800	23,900	26,400	28,400
1973	28,900	32,800	25,300	29,000	31,000
1974	32,000	35,800	27,700	32,300	34,800
1975	35,300	39,300	30,100	34,800	39,600
1976	38,100	41,800	32,900	36,500	46,100
1977	42,900	44,400	36,700	39,800	57,300
1978	48,700	47,900	42,200	45,100	66,700
1979	55,700	53,600	47,800	51,300	77,400
1980 (Sept.)	64,200	64,600	53,400	60,600	91,600
Percent Change 1970 to 1980	179.1%	156.3%	165.7%	173.0%	277.0%

Source: National Association of Realtors. *Existing Home Sales.* Washington, D.C.: Economics and Research Division, October, 1980.

declined quite sharply in the 1969 to 1973 period to between the 2.37 and 2.71 levels. After a brief return to the 2.9 mark from 1974 to 1976, the ratio abruptly soared; median sales prices now are substantially in excess of three times median family income as the decade of the 1980s commences. (The use of median family incomes, the reader should be reminded, tends to cloak very sharp and very meaningful variations. A reinspection of Exhibit 8 of chapter one is worthwhile in this context.)

The housing history of the last three decades has been one of enormous progress, of conversion of the bulk of America's households from renters to owners, and of a vast upgrading of the physical nature of the housing stock in all forms of tenure. This was accomplished in the earlier decades by a relatively positive relationship between the costs of acquiring housing and income levels. The last decade has been characterized by the very fact of inflation increasing housing values—precipitating additional housing demand even at the cost of obvious fiscal stress.

Facilitating this phenomenon has been the existence of fixed rate, long term mortgages in the face of inflationary pressures that clearly

EXHIBIT 3

Median Sales Prices of New One-Family Houses Sold and Median Family Income, United States: 1954 to 1979

Year	Median Sales Price	Median Family Income	Ratio of Sales Price to Income
1954	$12,300	$ 4,173	2.95
1955	13,700	4,421	3.10
1956	14,300	4,783	2.99
1959	15,200	5,417	2.81
1963	18,000	6,249	2.88
1964	18,900	6,569	2.88
1965	20,000	6,957	2.87
1966	21,400	7,532	2.84
1967	22,700	7,933	2.86
1968	24,700	8,632	2.86
1969	25,600	9,433	2.71
1970	23,400	9,867	2.37
1971	25,200	10,285	2.45
1972	27,600	11,116	2.48
1973	32,500	12,051	2.70
1974	35,900	12,836	2.78
1975	39,300	13,719	2.86
1976	44,200	14,958	2.95
1977	48,800	16,009	3.05
1978	55,700	17,640	3.16
1979	62,900	19,684	3.20

Source: U.S. Bureau of the Census, Department of Commerce. *Construction Reports*, "New One-Family Houses Sold and For Sale," Series C25-78-10. Washington, D.C.: U.S. Government Printing Office, December 1978. Also: Series C25-71-9, November 1971; C25-78-12, February 1978; and C25-80-7, September 1980. U.S. Bureau of the Census, Department of Commerce. Current Population Reports Series P-60, no. 125, *Money Income and Poverty Status of Families and Persons in the United States: 1979* (Advanced Report). Washington, D.C.: U.S. Government Printing Office, 1980.

have left those who supplied funds substantially less well off than those who borrowed them. The clarity with which this incongruity has surfaced makes it evident that this key factor *probably will not continue in the future.*

The 1980s will clearly mark the end of a fifty-year housing cycle, one in which America's shelter provisions became the envy of the world. They also will witness the maturation of a new phenomenon— the era of the scared American—the increasing belief that the future is not going to be as good as the past. Clearly, the housing "success" of the latter 70s can in part be attributed to such fears, of attempts to secure a stable port for the future via homeownership. Such motivations, and aspirations, are not likely to diminish casually; and their political repercussions will be proportional to the size of the population unable to board the "housing train."

Homeownership

An additional reference framework for viewing the deteriorating rent-income relationship is provided by the analogous financial shifts in the homeownership sector. Despite surging cost structures and obvious fiscal strictures, demand for homeownership continued to surge.

1. Between 1963 and 1970, the median sales price of new one-family homes sold in the United States increased by 30 percent; between 1970 and 1980, however, the median price soared by 186 percent. The same pattern of escalation is evidenced in the median prices of existing single-family homes sold.

2. One measure relating household income to shelter costs is the ratio of the median sales price of new one-family houses sold to median family income.

   (a) Through the 1950s and 1960s, the ratio fluctuated in the vicinity of 2.9.

   (b) In the early 1970s, as a result of a surge in production of federally subsidized ownership units, the ratio declined below the 2.5 level.

   (c) However, by 1975 the ratio had returned to its historic benchmark, i.e., approximately 2.9. But, a consistent rise was then evidenced in the ensuing years; by 1979 the sales price to income ratio reached the unprecedented level of 3.2.

3. Thus, the latter half of the 1970s witnessed a marked deterioration in the relationship between the costs of acquiring housing and income levels, a situation paralleling that of the rental market.

4. In contrast, however, the inflation in housing prices increased the demand for homeownership even at the cost of obvious fiscal stress, a tribute to the full emergence of the post-shelter society.

It is the parallel degeneration of the renter and ownership markets that adds complexity to the difficult questions about America's future shelter capacities in general, and rental housing's future in particular. The dilemmas that are both extant and imminent are considered in the final chapter.

6

Issues and Dilemmas

Chapters one and two have isolated the problems attendant to the key market sectors of rental housing: the household clientele burdened by high rent-income ratios. As projections have shown previously, such income deficient household configurations are destined to fall heir to the rental inventory as a result both of their absolute growth in number, as well as the vacating of the rental sector by more affluent husband-wife families. It is clear that rent paying capacity will be increasingly strained in the future.

Concurrently, the requirements of the stock to secure adequate financial inputs will certainly not abate. The harsh realities of the latter will be examined in the first two sections of this chapter: the issues of operating costs and the problem of financing costs. Other issues affecting the provision of rental housing are then examined: rent control, condominium conversion, and exclusionary zoning. Finally, the limited ability of the private market to grapple with these issues is considered, followed by the broader dilemmas of America's housing in the 1980s.

The Issue of Operating Costs

There is an unusual void in the nation's standardized data accounts in regard to the composition and changes in the operating cost structures of multifamily rental housing facilities. Despite the endemic crisis of growing imbalances between renter incomes and the costs of shelter, this situation has been permitted to continue. FHA operating cost data for rental structures, while informally accumulated in individual FHA offices, has yet to be coordinated, leaving the field with all too limited baselines.

83

Within this relative vacuum, there are two basic sources of operating information that provide some insight into the problem. The first is the "Price Index of Operating Costs for Rent Stabilized Apartment Houses," conducted for New York City and its Rent Stabilization Association by the Bureau of Labor Statistics. This index comprises a finite market basket of specifically defined operating elements; the changing prices of each element are tracked overtime, and by appropriately weighting each element—the fixed quantities of which were defined as of the time of the inception of this study in 1967—an overall price index is secured. While, by very definition the index is somewhat limited in its geographic range, its findings tend to be confirmed by the second study derived on a national base, which will be described later in this chapter.

Exhibits 1 and 2 summarize the experiences of the New York City "Price Index." From a base of 100 in 1967, the index experienced rapid increases to 132.2 by 1971 (Exhibit 2). The next five years, which incorporated the first energy crisis (1974), showed the index breaking the 200 level (203.5). Thus, by 1976, the terminal point of the first ten years of the index, a doubling of prices had been recorded. The ensuing four years, which once again incorporated an energy crisis, saw the index soar to the 270.3 level, despite a period of relative tranquility in 1978.

Thus, within a pattern of general increases, there were three distinct price surges: 1970 and 1971, 1973 and 1974, and most recently the 1979 to 1980 period. Interspersed between these surges are years of relatively mild price increases.

However, the latter often represent—at least within the political milieu of New York City—the politically feasible limits on rent increases. When exceptional increases are registered—such as 19.2 percent in 1974—the increment is often so large as to make it infeasible to adjust rents accordingly. Yet, it is virtually impossible (politically) to secure rent "catch-ups" in subsequent years, even ignoring limited rent paying capacities.

In Exhibit 1, the data are further dissected for the most recent five-year period, 1975 to 1980. It is noteworthy in this context to observe that even though taxes remained relatively constant with an increment of only 10.3 percent, every other element increased by nearly 40 percent or more. Fuel and utilities, as would be anticipated, nearly doubled (87.9 percent); insurance costs were the second most significant element, exhibiting an increase of nearly 60 percent.

The second set of data available on rental housing operating cost structures is provided by the Institute for Real Estate Management (IREM). This is an actual cost index rather than a price index. Since

EXHIBIT 1

Price Index of Operating Costs
for Rent Stabilized Apartment Houses,
New York City: 1975 to 1980
(1967 = 100)

Group	1975	1980	Change: 1975 to 1980	
			Number	Percent
All items	191.3	270.3	79.0	41.3%
Taxes, fees, and permits	153.6	169.4	15.8	10.3
Labor costs	208.4	291.6	83.2	39.9
Fuel and utilities	345.1	648.5	303.4	87.9
Contractor services	180.3	255.1	74.8	41.5
Administrative costs	142.5	200.4	57.9	40.6
Insurance costs	206.8	330.6	123.8	59.9
Parts and supplies	181.7	267.2	85.5	47.1
Replacement costs	148.0	212.5	64.5	43.6

Source: U.S. Department of Labor, Bureau of Labor Statistics, Middle Atlantic Regional Office. *1980 Price Index of Operating Costs for Rent Stabilized Apartment Houses in New York City,* Annual.

a fixed market basket is not adhered to, a cost index reflects actual operating experience, i.e., undoubtedly mirroring efforts of owners to reduce, or find substitutes for, specifically costly operational elements. Unfortunately, at this writing, the most current data is available only from 1975 through 1978. (In order to provide comparability, note that on the bottom of Exhibit 2 the New York City experience from 1975 to 1978 is also isolated.) Nonetheless, as shown in Exhibit 3, over the four-year period—regardless of specific configuration, whether elevator, low rise, or garden—the cost experience reflected double digit inflation roughly comparable to the price increases gauged in New York City (Exhibit 2). Garden apartment units were the least impacted, but even here there was an increase of 13.2 percent.

Exhibit 3 further details a comparison of changes in gross rents per square foot that took place using the IREM sample in the same period from 1975 to 1978. Rent gains, in general, exceeded the increments in costs. This is detailed at the bottom of the exhibit that isolates changes in the annual operating ratios from 1975 to 1978—operating expenses divided by rent collections.

But, this was the result of a number of years in which operating costs were decidedly restrained. Referring back again to the 1975 to 1978 period, as shown in Exhibit 2, the cumulative impact of inflation in those several years averaged out to less than 5-percent

THE FUTURE OF RENTAL HOUSING

EXHIBIT 2

Price Index of Operating Costs for Rent Stabilized Apartment Houses, New York City: 1967 to 1980

Year (As of April)	Index	Percent Change
1967	100.0	—
1968	103.5	3.5
1969	107.6	4.0
1970	116.6	8.4
1971	132.2	13.4
1972	139.7	5.7
1973	150.8	7.9
1974	179.7	19.2
1975	191.3	6.5
1976	203.5	6.4
1977	219.5	7.9
1978	220.5	0.5
1979	238.6	8.2
1980	270.3	13.3

The 1975 to 1978 Period

			Change: 1975 to 1978	
1975	1978		Number	Percent
191.3	220.5		29.2	15.3%

The 1978 to 1980 Period

			Change: 1978 to 1980	
1978	1980		Number	Percent
220.5	270.3		49.8	22.6%

Source: U.S. Department of Labor, Bureau of Labor Statistics, Middle Atlantic Regional Office. *1980 Price Index of Operating Costs for Rent Stabilized Apartment Houses in New York City*, Annual.

per year. If, on the other hand, the 1978 to 1980 period is examined (Exhibit 2), the hammer blow of inflation in costs—increasing 22.6 percent in New York City in this brief period—becomes evident.

The specific components of the cost increases from 1975 to 1978 are shown in subsequent exhibits. Without going into detail on the individual elements, it is evident that they represent a very broad spectrum of expenditure requirements.

Thus, in sum, operating costs, assuming a finite market basket, have nearly tripled (following the New York experience) from 1967 through 1980. Despite landlords' efforts to alter the market basket of expense items, and thus minimize the impact of individual item cost increments, the national data (IREM) tend to suggest that the New York experience is not atypical.

The last three years, 1978 to 1980, have shown the most marked increment. Earlier shocks of cost surges were typically confined to a single year. We now suffer from a cumulative impact. Landlords in the broad, from 1975 to 1978, were able to raise rents in a fashion more than adequate to cope with expense inflation in these years. However, given the income characteristic of renters, particularly in the central city, the stresses of most recent years need little elaboration. But, even this measure of rent gains probably overstates their salubrious effect. Rents tend to lag behind expenses—note very specifically the enormous level of increment in the latter in the 1973 to 1974 period. To that degree the improvement in operating ratios from 1975 to 1978 (shown on the bottom of Exhibit 3) probably is illusory.

The Problem of Financing Costs

The expenditure patterns described above refer only to operating costs. They do not take into account the enormous shifts that have taken place in capital costs. And these have been even more brutal in their impact both on investor interest in extant apartment houses as well as the development of new ones. The old rule of thumb of a new building being worth somewhere on the order of seven times the rent roll clearly can make very little sense when the mortgage costs of the finished structure exceed the 14-percent level—and that is effectively the case today. Owners of older buildings, even with much lower rate mortgages, find themselves—and their equity—trapped by the increments in interest rates, unless very substantial rent increases are forthcoming. If, for example, we assume an older building only valued at five times the rent roll, the situation becomes clear. If the owner wishes to remortgage a paid down indenture, which may have been written at the 9-percent mark, at a time when interest rates are at the 13-percent level, the increment in interest costs is roughly equal to 20 percent of the rent roll (i.e., 4 percent multiplied by five times the building's rent roll). In conversations with developers, the phrase very frequently used that there is no more "leverage" in building finance: that the yields on equity for new multifamily residential facilities may not exceed that given to debt.

The limitations on expending rents are severe. They are exacerbated, but far from limited to the constraints of rent control. Much more formidable, much more widespread, and much more chronic,

EXHIBIT 3

General Operating Parameters: 1975 to 1978

Median Operating Expenses Per Square Foot, 1975 to 1978: USA and Canada				
			Change: 1975 to 1978	
Building Type	1975	1978	Number	Percent
Elevator	$1.92	$2.26	$.34	17.7%
Low Rise, 25+ Units	1.40	1.76	.36	25.7
Low Rise, 12 to 24 Units	1.37	1.59	.22	16.1
Garden	1.29	1.46	.17	13.2

Gross Rent Per Square Foot, 1975 to 1978: USA and Canada				
			Change: 1975 to 1978	
Building Type	1975	1978	Number	Percent
Elevator	$3.32	$4.11	$.79	23.7%
Low Rise, 25+ Units	2.93	3.55	.62	21.2
Low Rise, 12 to 24 Units	2.87	3.50	.63	22.0
Garden	2.57	3.09	.52	20.2

Annual Operating Ratio 1975 to 1978: USA and Canada (Operating Expenses ÷ Rent Collections)				
			Change: 1975 to 1978	
Building Type	1975	1978	Number	Percent
Elevator	55.8%	53.7%	2.1%	−3.8%
Low Rise, 25+ Units	49.3	48.6	0.7	−1.4
Low Rise, 12 to 24 Units	49.3	45.3	4.0	−8.1
Garden	51.8	47.6	4.2	−8.1

Source: IREM, Income/Expense Analysis. Chicago: Institute of Real Estate Management, 1979.

is the increasing paucity of rent paying capacity of renter households as shown earlier in this study.

Indeed, if one were to use current mortgage costs, there is very little real equity left in the field of conventional rental ownership. It has been implicitly wiped out by the increases in the effective costs of debt required for sale or refinancing.

While certainly nonresidential facilities have been impacted by the same phenomenon, typically there is either a much greater capacity to pass on rent increments to their ultimate customers—

EXHIBIT 4

Operating Expenses: 1975 to 1978
Elevator Buildings
(Median Dollars Per Square Foot)

	1975	1978	Change: 1975 to 1978	
			Number	Percent
TOTAL EXPENSES	$1.92	$2.26	$.34	17.7%
Administrative	.20	.29	.09	45.0
Management Costs	.15	.22	.07	46.7
Other Administrative Expenses	.04	.04	.00	0.0
Operating	.49	.66	.17	34.7
Supplies	.02	.02	.00	0.0
Heating Fuel	.16	.30	.14	87.5
Electricity	.15	.33	.18	120.0
Water/Sewer	.05	.06	.01	20.0
Gas	.03	.05	.02	66.7
Building Services	.03	.03	.00	0.0
Other	.02	.02	.00	0.0
Maintenance	.25	.42	.17	68.0
Taxes and Insurance	.59	.75	.16	27.1
Other	.23	.26	.03	13.0

Source: IREM. *Income/Expense Analysis.* Chicago: Institute of Real Estate Management, 1979.

as, for example, in a shopping center—or it represents a relatively small part of the overall operating statement of the firm—the prestige office headquarters building. There is no such buffer when we turn to the bulk of the residential renter market.

In addition, it should be noted that the concept of the renegotiable mortgage, while something of a novelty in private residential financing, has long been used de facto in multifamily housing. Thus, nongovernmental mortgages in the field have been typically written for relatively short periods of time, though based upon long-term amortization. This permitted lending institutions to review the satisfactoriness of the payment experience as well as interest rates. While, historically, this was a relatively passive process, in terms of rates, it currently means that the renegotiation process is much more onerous than those accustomed to long-term fixed rate borrowing may appreciate.

EXHIBIT 5

Operating Expenses: 1975 to 1978
Low Rise, Over 24 Units
(Median Dollars Per Square Foot)

	1975	1978	Change: 1975 to 1978 Number	Percent
TOTAL EXPENSES	$1.40	$1.76	$.36	25.7%
Administrative	.15	.24	.09	60.0
Management Costs	.13	.21	.08	61.5
Other Administrative Expenses	.04	.04	.00	0.0
Operating	.34	.45	.11	32.4
Supplies	.02	.02	.00	0.0
Heating Fuel	.13	.22	.09	69.2
Electricity	.06	.18	.12	200.0
Water/Sewer	.05	.07	.02	40.0
Gas	.04	.04	.00	0.0
Building Services	.04	.04	.00	0.0
Other	.01	.02	.01	100.0
Maintenance	.19	.29	.10	52.6
Taxes and Insurance	.52	.60	.80	153.8
Other	.19	.18	−.01	−5.2

Source: IREM. *Income/Expense Analysis.* Chicago: Institute of Real Estate Management, 1979.

Thus, the substitution of government lending for these purposes is in part a tribute to the availability of the latter; it also reflects on the necessity for fixed interest rates over long periods of time— and these are largely available only from the nonprivate sector.

For the sake of brevity, we have not discussed here the changing balanced cost of capital as equity is further squeezed. It should be noted, however, that in general the proportion of total value that will be covered by a mortgage lender on a multifamily residential facility has shown some signs of decreasing over time, i.e., requiring much more in the way of relatively expensive equity participation. In general, government lending has been much more generous in terms of its coverage.

In sum, therefore, the construction of new multifamily residential facilities is substantially hindered by a rate of inflation in operating costs that is not matched by the rent paying capacity of the tenantry.

EXHIBIT 6

Operating Expenses: 1975 to 1978
Low Rise, Over 24 Units
(Median Dollars Per Square Foot)

	1975	1978	Change: 1975 to 1978 Number	Percent
TOTAL EXPENSES	$1.37	$1.59	$.22	16.1%
Administrative	.17	.20	.03	17.6
Management Costs	.14	.18	.04	28.6
Other Administrative Expenses	.03	.02	−.01	−33.3
Operating	.30	.41	.11	36.7
Supplies	.01	.02	.01	100.0
Heating Fuel	.14	.27	.13	92.9
Electricity	.05	.08	.03	60.0
Water/Sewer	.05	.06	.01	20.0
Gas	.04	.06	.02	50.0
Building Services	.04	.05	.01	25.0
Other	.01	.02	.01	100.0
Maintenance	.18	.34	.16	88.9
Taxes and Insurance	.54	.58	.04	7.4
Other	.12	.16	.04	33.3

Source: IREM. *Income/Expense Analysis.* Chicago: Institute of Real Estate Management, 1979.

It is further accentuated by the increased costs of capital and borrowing. Again, these latter two elements have little in the way of buffering potential (except for luxury buildings), in terms of pass through to the tenantry. Government has become not merely the lender of the last resort, typically limited to the specifically impacted, but rather the primary source of multifamily rental structure finance. And, this will not change.

These limitations and requirements take on increased significance as we turn to the issues of placing all housing and its related financial requirements within a context of an economy that for the moment seems increasingly at sea.

Housing Versus Reindustrialization: New Priorities

One of the visions that haunts efforts at projecting housing realities into the future is one of a splendid tract development

EXHIBIT 7

Operating Expenses: 1975 to 1978
Garden Type Buildings
(Median Dollars Per Square Foot)

	1975	1978	Change: 1975 to 1978 Number	Percent
TOTAL EXPENSES	$1.29	$1.46	$.17	13.2%
Administrative	.17	.26	.09	52.9
Management Costs	.13	.19	.06	46.2
Other Administrative Expenses	.04	.05	.01	25.0
Operating	.27	.38	.11	40.7
Supplies	.01	.02	.01	100.0
Heating Fuel	.11	.19	.08	72.7
Electricity	.06	.22	.16	266.7
Water/Sewer	.06	.09	.03	50.0
Gas	.03	.07	.04	133.3
Building Services	.03	.03	.00	0.0
Other	.01	.02	.01	100.0
Maintenance	.19	.32	.13	68.4
Taxes and Insurance	.33	.38	.05	15.2
Other	.17	.17	.00	0.0

Source: IREM. Income/Expense Analysis. Chicago: Institute of Real Estate Management, 1979.

surrounding an abandoned factory. The issue of whether America can afford a pattern of increased housing investment, at the very same time that the requirements of defense—and of reindustrialization—come to the fore, has yet to be adequately answered. At present, the issues are just beginning to be defined. It is evident, however, that some of the "easy answers" have already been exhausted, and may have even precipitated new crises of their own. For example, as of this writing, the sheer volume of municipal and state housing authority bond issues has yielded a situation in which prime offerings require interest rates of 12 percent, thus yielding effective subsidized mortgage instruments at upwards of the 13-percent level.

The costs of this pressure on the federal fisc, both directly in terms of foregone taxes and indirectly in terms of crowding in the bond market, need little elaboration. In addition, where once federal government guarantees on borrowing instruments provided a salient subsidy for housing purposes, this is decreasingly the case. In 1979 alone, the federal government authorized well in excess of $100 billion of such indentures for a variety of purposes. The market has grown less and less responsive as a consequence of the unrelenting wave of such instruments.

The issue of increasing savings levels among Americans, and further the question of whether such saving should be encouraged for housing as against investment in industrial infrastructure, are currently being debated in the halls of Congress. In the last three years, however, we have nearly completely shattered the hitherto sheltered status of housing finance and the institutions that have acted as intermediaries in providing this goal. The invention of the certificate of deposit and the philosophy behind its issuance, as well as the continuous blurring of the unique character of thrift institutions, has consciously, or otherwise, obliterated the preferential treatment that housing has secured over the last fifty years. It is extremely difficult to conceive that the historic parameters will be restored in any substantial fashion.

Impact of Rent Control on the Provision of Rental Housing

Rent control is both a finite phenomenon in terms of its direct impact on rental housing, as well as representing the pinnacle of changes in landlord/tenant relationships and legal standing.

The impact on new construction of the first element is very clearcut. In a time of inflation, owners and lenders simply are not willing to venture into areas in which the absolute rents (as well as rates of return) will be limited. While efforts have been made in this context to make the particular strictures of control mechanisms more generous than held true in the past, at best these are rarely considered as dependable; at worst, they are construed as simply insufficient.

Even if a satisfactory first rent level can be achieved for new construction, there is the onerous threat of future constraints not matching the realities of the market. The operation of extant units falls under a somewhat similar cloud. Again, if at present there is an adequate rate of return, there is a limited potential for capital accumulation as a result of upgrading, since typically the provisions for recapturing the costs of capital improvements (and with them increased rents) are drastically limited.

It should further be noted that the threat of rent control may be nearly as inhibitory to investment as its reality. Thus, the normal vagaries of development are made even more riskful by either the presence or potential presence of control mechanisms—the higher the risk, the higher the rate of return required for investment.

It is the second element, however—of basic changes in landlord/ tenant relationships in many jurisdictions—that are no less dramatic, and perhaps have an even greater significance in altering the investment appeal of conventional rental facilities. The old commitment of the English common law to the provision of four bare walls has given way to a great complexity of requirements levied on the owner. While these may be far overdue—and certainly in many cases far from adequate in terms of habitability—they diminish the arm's length nature of the investment, requiring much more in the way of management inputs and much more in the way of adjudication of tenant responses. "If you don't like it, move!" is, in most jurisdictions, a phrase viewed with melancholy by owners.

Without detailing the merits of this new balance, suffice it to say that it has brought in its wake a great change in investment behavior. For example, insurance companies currently desperate for real estate investment as a hedge against inflation, are not anxious to be viewed in the new unpopular light of apartment owners. The dangers of much publicized tenant picketing, or complaints, worthy as their antecedents may be, simply raise the break even point of entry to investors with alternative outlets.

Increasingly, therefore, investment capital has avoided the conventional field of multifamily rental housing. Such strictures are not as vital to comparatively small operations and operators. Thus, in the place of specifically built for rent developments, a variety of alternative approaches and mechanisms have come into being: the subdivision of one-family homes and with it the provision of rental facilities, as well as the purchase for investment of individual condominium units with a subsequent or parallel rental. Typically, these are units that do not fall under rent control provisions, or are provided within an investment/management context that minimizes conflict.

It is the public sector that falls heir to the vacuum left behind by private investment. The last decade has seen a process familiar to those who have worked in New York City—the replacement of purely private market financing and development to one largely dominated by government underwriting. In the words of one investor: "If it stands, it's mine—if it falls, it's the FHAs."

The Rise of the Condominium

The HUD study of the conversion of rental housing to condominiums and cooperatives has left little need for elaboration. Suffice it to say that the net impact of the processes at work on the rental housing industry in terms of net losses to the rental market is relatively trivial (see Appendix B).

What may be even more pertinent, however, is the fact that just at the time that the classic tract house as an alternative to rental facilities moves out of the fiscal reach of many would be home-buyers, it is replaced by the hybred mechanisms of individual owner-ship in multifamily units. The condominium/co-op movement, therefore, may be viewed as most significant in terms of furthering the cream-skimming process earlier referred to, i.e., the pulling out of the rental market of the more affluent who choose ownership, even of compromise forms, in the light of the inflationary induced tax advantages that are attached to it.

Exclusionary Zoning

The attitude of zoning boards toward multifamily housing for rental purposes vary substantially across the country. For example, at a time in which most of the Northeast literally had no land zoned for such purposes, the mid-West, particularly in the greater Chicago area, probably had excessive acreage devoted to this nominal pur-pose. In general, however, most zoning practices have restrained the development at relatively high densities of multifamily units. Con-ventional standards in many areas of great demand (where such land is available) limit development to no more than a half-dozen units per acre.

In the Northeast, the bulk of development still requires a variance, i.e., a rather expensive, often time consuming and—even if successful—riskful procedure, rather than development of these much needed facilities as a matter of right. The results, in terms of increments in per-unit land costs, need little elaboration.

The failure of states to exercise their prerogatives in land develop-ment, and the virtually complete absence of the federal government in this regard, still severely limit the areas in which rental units can be built and, even more stringently, where they can be built relatively *cheaply.*

Adjudicating the Balance Between Supply and Demand

In retrospect, the decade of the 1970s started off with a relatively low level of inflation, which quickly accelerated to our present anticipation of a "base" plateau on the order of 9 percent. While the general acknowledgment of this underlying level may be challenged, there is clear evidence that it is now built into the consumer's mind. Thus, the movement from rental facilities to homeownership may be seen initially as a classic reflection of increased housing buying power, but in its latter stages it is reflected of the "post-shelter" housing market—one in which housing is seen as a protective device (and indeed a very rare one) against the ravages of inflation.

As a consequence, it is very largely those elements of our society who cannot obtain homeownership, who are the principal factors and growth elements in the rental housing market. The factors at work in the future—the balance between the capacity for home-ownership, the post-inflation real "costs" of shelter, and potential changes in tax laws; all of which must be factored into the equation—make definitive forecasts uncertain at best. One of the parameters that can provide some measure of clarification is the potential provision of financing.

Much has been made of the difficulties in securing private home mortgages. While a whole host of new instruments have been de-vised, all of them essentially depend upon further inflation in the value of the house in order to provide an actuarially sound base. The realities of their adoption in the market, their potential for warning away new homebuyers and the like, still must meet the test of experience.

In addition, the nation's financial resources will be required to meet the challenge of alternative areas of lending and indeed of equity participation. It is evident, once again at least within the short-term future, that nonhousing elements will secure the bulk of tax preferential treatment. While some measures to enhance the desirability of conventional savings in thrift institutions through lower tax payments for some measure of interest are promising, the pressures will continue.

Moreover, it is highly questionable whether our economy as a whole can support a level of inflation that has minimized the real cost of borrowing for housing purposes. If we are truly to cope with inflation, the costs of nonnecessary borrowing must be much higher than the rewards.

While one can hope that once some measure of stability is restored, a less primitive philosophy will prevail; but this clearly is going to take a rather lengthy period of time. In the interim, long-term fixed rate mortgages will remain in their death throes, and the post-shelter society will be aborted. Volatile economic conditions to which we have become accustomed virtually dictate mortgage instruments that can swiftly and adequately reflect, and adjust to, sharp changes in the broader economic environment.

Difficult as is the situation for single homes, it is comparatively mild compared to the situation faced by apartment developers. These center around the even gloomier prospect for conventional mortgage instruments with which to finance rental facilities.

The sum of our study has been to indicate the declining interest in rental facilities by the more affluent in our society—those presently with the greatest rent paying capacity, and prospectively with the greatest level of increments in income. Their replacement has largely been concentrated among those of more limited rent paying resources, and with much less in the way of incremental income potential. In the face of these demand factors, the vulnerability of conventional mortgage finance instruments to rental housing—or even the new semi-indexed instrumentalities—is all too evident. To reiterate a previous example, if we assume a not overly optimistic mortgage that represents five times the rent roll, envision the problem if the same instrument is renegotiable by contract every three years, and faces a not improbable increment of 4 percent in the interest rate. This would necessitate an increase, just for the purposes of interest service, of approximately 20 percent (five times the rent role times 4 percent). With the exception of an occasional luxury building, or one whose servicing costs are guaranteed by the federal government, it is difficult to envision either entrepreneurs on the one hand, or mortgage lenders on the other, anxious to embark on such uncertain requirements.

Instead, we do not have to envision the future—in part it is with us. In the condominium/co-op, we very largely have a substitution of personal credit for the collateral value of the collective entity: the building. The latter, under a renter tenurial form, simply is too open to the ravages of inflation and the higher real costs following these effects, as well as the impact of progressive income taxes on tenants of affluence. By moving into the modified ownership form, we substitute individual incomes, individual credit, individual capacity to raise the wherewithal for the conventional collateral of the building. And we further buffer such individual borrowers through current tax law as well as the potential of inflationary increments.

Thus, interpreting demographic trends according to the conventional market wisdom of the 1960s would indicate substantial increases in rental tenure, our projections (chapter 2) do not see this as forthcoming. If anything, we would suggest that the rental demand estimates may well be on the optimistic side. Their achievement will virtually depend exclusively on the provision of federal mortgage funding—or rent supplementation.

Rental-Condominium Linkages

There are a variety of potentials to the condominium format that, particularly in terms of broadening financial markets, are just coming into sight. As Appendix B indicates, a rather substantial

number of apartment units that have been converted to condominium form are not owner occupied—but rather continued as
rental facilities, with the tax and potential value increases secured
by an absentee investor.

A number of variations are possible on this theme as we unbundle
the package of rights and privileges that differentiate rental facilities
from those of ownership. At this writing, several public syndicates
have been projected to build conventional nongovernment financed
rental housing units. The debt financing for this purpose is secured
through a public flotation. The bonus attributes, which permit
relatively low interest rates, are secured not only by the promise of
tax cover (far from a novelty as, for example, in the earlier limited
partnerships), but also participation in rent increases, and, most
strikingly of all, a premeditated projection of conversion to condominium status, typically in the seventh to tenth year.

While the practice of utilizing the tax virtues of rental housing in
order to secure participation of those in tax brackets to whom this
is valuable is far from unique, when these allures are further broadened
by condominium conversion potential, the latter may be viewed
increasingly as a stimulus to rental housing construction rather than
an inevitable detractor.

It is in this area of relatively inexpensive, modest condominiums,
secured both through conversion as well as new construction that
offers the potential of absorbing much of the friction of declining
housing buying power in America's future.

But, it should be noted in this context, that while this may produce both shelter and ultimately housing investment opportunities
for the middle incomed, it by no means can provide an adequate
bridge across the gap between the rent paying capacities of the poor
and the necessities of new rental housing. And, it is in this seemingly
irreducible last area that government's role as a housing supporter
"of last resort" cannot be denied.

In the absence of these instrumentalities we do not foresee a
capacity on the part of the private market to deliver the required
rental facilities. The penalties imposed on the lower incomed will
involve, at the least, a reversal of the progress made against overcrowding, as well as a conversion of marginal individual facilities
into housing for two or more households.

Impending Dilemmas

The aggregate of the preceding discussions (as well as the analyses
in the previous chapters) point to a hazy but troubled housing
future. Before examining some of the more critical elements that

we see emerging, it is useful to again review the events of the most recent past. Indeed, it is possible to consider the 1970s as signalling the end of the golden housing era.

The housing history of the last three decades has been one of enormous progress, of conversion of the bulk of America's households from renters to owners, and of a vast upgrading of the physical nature of the housing stock in all forms of tenure. But, the era that peaked in the 1970s appears to have come to an end as the 1980s commence.

1. In retrospect, the 1970s was clearly a period in which an unprecedented housing dynamic was forged. Surging housing production and unparalleled household formation proceeded hand in hand to virtually reshape the aspirations of American society.

2. The final audits of the decade's housing ledgers will show America's housing inventory expanding by about 17-million units, an increment over 60-percent greater than that achieved in any intercensal decade.

3. This phenomenon was paralleled by an incredible surge in household formation as America's population rapidly partitioned itself into an increasing number of smaller and varied household formats. While these demographic shifts possessed substantial internal momentum, their surfacing was certainly facilitated by the sheer expansion of the housing supply.

4. The 1970s will also be remembered as a period of homeownership aspirations—and fulfillment. This was accomplished in the beginning of the decade by a relatively positive relationship between the costs of acquiring housing and income levels. The end of the decade was characterized by the very fact of inflation increasing housing values—precipitating additional housing demand even at the cost of obvious fiscal stress.

5. The latter marked the maturation of the post-shelter society, a phenomenon unique in its depth to our own time. The long-term chronic inflation of the 1970s altered behavior with equivalent vigor. Housing in America became much more important as a form of investment, as a form of forced savings, and as a refuge from inflation rather than from the elements.

6. The consequence to the rental market—the cream-skimming of the more affluent tenantry into homeownership—raised serious question as to the long-term economic rationales

underpinning rental housing. It also brought into focus the growing income imbalances between owners and renters, as well as across the profile of household types.

7. The housing success of the 1970s and the post-shelter society was facilitated by mortgage instrumentalities—designed for stable noninflationary economic environments—extending into a period characterized by strikingly new contours. Fixed rate mortgages, inadequately reflecting volatile economic conditions, made housing borrowing an unprecedented bargain.

8. But, those who supplied funds were left substantially less well off than those who borrowed them. The clarity with which this incongruity has surfaced makes it evident that this key factor will not continue in the future, that forecasting America's housing cannot simply be an extrapolation of demographics, using the same linkages that have prevailed in the past.

As we look to the 1980s, the historical events of the late 1970s presage some immediate dilemmas. Key among these are our preliminary future demand estimates, to which we can raise serious question.

9. Employing the conventional wisdom of future household formation, as well as extrapolations of 1970 to 1980 tenure patterns, "first approximation" demand projections indicate net gains of 4.1-million renter households and 12.7-million owner households over the decade of the 1980s—growth totals comparable in magnitude to those recorded during its predecessor.

10. However, the "calibration" of the projection model is based upon a historic period of relative affluence within which rapid household formation and fragmentation were facilitated by the availability of relatively inexpensive housing. This phenomenon is not likely to be easily replicated in the coming decade; as the real costs of housing escalate, the process of household formation will decelerate.

Indeed, the latter potential will be heightened by the ominous trends in income variations and financing realities.

11. The process of income segmentation—of sharp income variations by household type and configuration—will probably accelerate over the course of the decade. While real income gains on an aggregate basis will be minimal, the reservoir of

two-income households is still being filled, and represents a new partition in America's class structure. This group may well secure the affluence to board the "housing train." Conversely, a much more serious problem—obscured by the sheer size of the baby boom generation's aspirations—centers on female headed families, particularly among minority groups, whose income resources are so deficient as to be noneffective in the housing market.

12. Between these two extremes lies a population whose incomes will fail to keep pace with the costs of shelter. The basic issue is whether American can afford to provide housing at the scale and variety of configurations that we have grown to accept as our right.

13. The financing variable of the housing market equation will have to meet the challenge of alternative areas of lending and indeed of equity participation. Reindustrialization versus housing may become a confrontation of significant proportions as the nation explicitly considers whether it can afford a pattern of increased housing investment.

14. Implicitly, the demise of long-term fixed rate housing finance already serves as an indicator of emerging priorities: the costs of nonessential borrowing must be higher than the rewards. The new instrumentalities—variable rate and shared appreciation formats—serve this end, but in turn signal the reduction of housing's unique national priority.

15. The 1980s may well turn out to be an era of "shock-cushioning"—of adapting the expectations of consumers to the new realities of housing costs. Whether cloaked by the euphemisms of "townhouses" or "villas," the reality will be one of masking reduced quality.

Appendix A
The Maintenance of America's
Housing Stock*

The Attrition of America's Housing Stock

The concept of scrappage rate, the proportion of a user inventory that is removed on an annual basis, is a very familiar one in most areas of American business. There are few individuals involved in the industry, for example, who are not familiar with the fact that the half life (the length of time before half of a model year's production is retired from use) of washing machines is eight years, that the equivalent for automobiles slightly less than that, etc. This is a backbone element in all projections made by market forecasters. Indeed, changes in the scrappage rate, i.e., the obsolescence of gas-guzzling cars, or the introduction of a new model that suddenly makes a previous appliance obsolete, may be far more significant to total market demand than are new users per se. It is striking in this context to note the lack of use of the same conceptual apparatus when we turn to housing. And, this is in the face of a current scrappage rate that approximates 1 percent of the stock per year. As best we can estimate it, we are currently losing between 600-and 800-thousand housing units per year. At present levels of removal, therefore, the

*Prepared for the Office of the Secretary, Department of Housing and Urban Development, by George Sternlieb, 1980.

half life of America's housing inventory would be approximately fifty years (i.e., half of the extant stock would be removed from use in half a century).

To a very substantial degree the level of scrappage is a tribute to post-World War II housing production mechanisms that have provided an irregular but relatively powerful stream of new units to the pool of extant housing—and thus has permitted the removal of units that either in their absolute age and obsolescence, or sometimes in configuration, are no longer of utility. In increasing measure, however, we are grudgingly becoming aware of the phenomenon of abandonment for less salubrious reasons: because of neighborhood problems, failures of the market and maintenance, and a variety of other variables.

When the housing buying power of Americans was at the peak reached within the last generation, this occasioned relatively little alarm. However, as we see the replacement costs of new units soaring, the demand for a more rational approach to the housing market becomes much more insistent. The limitations of attempting to provide new units for people with relatively low housing buying power, whether in rental or homeownership, are evident from the charges engendered by Section 8. It is important here to indicate that the soaring costs involved make the preservation of the low rental stock far more important to the nation as a whole than has hitherto been the case. In many cases, we simply will not be able to afford to provide new housing in sufficient quantities and at appropriate prices to replace some of the units that are potentially of value, but which are slipping from the stock.

The Broad National/Regional Overview

In four years, from 1973 to 1977, more than 1.1-million units that had been owner occupied in 1973 were removed from the stock, an additional 1.5-million renter occupied units suffered the same fate, as did over a half-million units that were vacant in 1973. In a brief period of four years there was a loss in excess of 3-million housing units in a universe of approximately 75 million; thus, approximately one out of every 25 units in the United States that was extant in 1973 had been scrapped by 1977.

The removal was most forcefully evident in terms of units that had been vacant in 1973—nearly 10 percent (9.7%) of these units were removed. Owner occupied housing, as would be guessed, suffered least from this type of attrition with a removal rate of only 2.5 percent over the four years. Renter occupied units, however, fared harshly with slightly over 1.5 million, or 6.3 percent of the 1973 inventory removed.

In general, this impacted black occupied housing units—whether owned or rented—much more than was the case for their white equivalents, with nearly twice the proportion of black as white occupied rental units disappearing from the inventory, while one and a half times the proportion of owner occupied units suffered the same fate (see Exhibit 1).

The nature of the dual housing market is discussed separately; it must be stressed that this selective demolition certainly impacts much more forcefully on the inventory of "black" housing units than it does of whites. Thus, to the degree that blacks are limited to finding shelter in the set of previously black occupied housing units, the pressures upon them of this selective removal from the stock are far more onerous than holds true for the majority group.

Regional Variation

There is substantial regional variation in the incidence and kind of removal from the stock that took place. Owner occupied housing in the Northeast, for example, had the greatest level of stability with only 1.4 percent of it being removed in the four years under consideration. The South was highest in this regard with a figure of 3.6 percent, with the North Central at 2.1, and the West intermediate at 2.3.

It is in rental housing, however, where the variation in regional levels of attrition becomes truly significant. It is the South once again that is in the lead in this characteristic with a loss of 7.5 percent, i.e., nearly one in fourteen of its 1973 rental units. The Northeast is second in this category with a loss of 5.9 percent of its occupied rental units—and an even more striking loss of 11.9 percent: one out of nine—of its black occupied units.

Regardless of region, it is the rental facilities that generally have taken the brunt of the removal syndrome. The North Central states with their industrial cities carrying the heaviest burden, suffered the greatest attrition of renter occupied units—even more so than in the Northeast—with a loss of 6.4 percent or one out of sixteen units. Among black occupied units the attrition rate is an even more striking 13.5 percent, or more than one in eight.

The point should be emphasized that the absolute bulk of the units that were removed from the 1973 stock had been occupied in that base year. While certainly the proportion of attrition was highest in vacant year round units—and one may surmise that many of them were vacant because they were simply not competitive within the market—the greater part of the removals were units that,

EXHIBIT 1

Occupancy Status by Region and Race of 1973 Housing Units Removed from the Inventory by 1977
(in thousands)

Region, Race Occupancy Status	Total 1973 Units	Total 1973 Units Removed by 1977	% of 1973 Units Removed by 1977
National			
Owner Occupied	44,653	1,108	2.5
White	41,239	986	2.4
Black	3,024	113	3.7
Renter Occupied	24,684	1,552	6.3
White	20,224	1,117	5.5
Black	3,938	400	10.0
Vacant, Year Round	5,956	575	9.7
Northeast			
Owner Occupied	9,555	133	1.4
White	9,117	126	1.4
Black	385	7	1.8
Renter Occupied	6,597	392	5.9
White	5,543	274	4.9
Black	922	110	11.9
Vacant, Year Round	1,239	88	7.1
North Central			
Owner Occupied	12,945	276	2.1
White	12,264	246	2.0
Black	639	29	4.5
Renter Occupied	5,797	372	6.4
White	4,913	254	5.2
Black	812	110	13.5
Vacant, Year Round	1,437	175	12.2
South			
Owner Occupied	14,498	523	3.6
White	12,723	448	3.5
Black	1,717	72	4.2
Renter Occupied	7,307	550	7.5
White	5,415	383	7.1
Black	1,824	164	9.0
Vacant, Year Round	2,163	245	11.3
West			
Owner Occupied	7,655	176	2.3
White	7,135	165	2.3
Black	284	6	2.1
Renter Occupied	4,983	237	4.8
White	4,353	205	4.7
Black	380	16	4.2
Vacant, Year Round	1,118	67	6.0

Source: *Annual Housing Survey:* 1973, Series H-150-73A.
1977, Series H-150-77.

for better or worse, had been providing shelter for tenantry, both owner and renter.

Is their removal a tribute to the improvements of the overall ambiance of housing—of greater housing availability generally or does it stem from a variety of elements—and some of them far less salubrious?

Detailing the Scrapped Housing Condition

The vast bulk of the 1973 housing stock that suffered attrition did not lack plumbing facilities, but rather had complete bathrooms, complete kitchens, and appropriate central heating facilities. Nor, in general, were they drastically overcrowded as of the base line observation year.

Our information on the characteristics of units removed from the inventory is far from as complete as might be desired. In the several exhibits that follow, we have attempted to summarize some of the data.

Size of Structure

In Exhibit 2, the number of housing units extant in 1973 that were removed from the housing inventory by 1977 are shown, by size of the structure in which they were located. In general, the phenomenon has been most striking in relatively small scale, renter occupied structures, with an attrition rate of one in sixteen of all renter occupied units in structures with four or fewer units. The equivalent for larger structures runs slightly over the 4-percent level, i.e., a shade over one in twenty-five.

The attrition rate in owner occupied units is much lower in absolute scale, the size of the universe of owner occupied units in larger scaled buildings is relatively small. The data are therefore somewhat fragmentary and much more subject to error. For what little it may be worth, however, there is a reverse phenomenom, i.e., the one-family owner occupied unit is much less subject to removal from the stock than the multifamily equivalent.

The Age of Structures Removed from the Housing Inventory

In Exhibit 3, there is a comparison of the total inventory by age of America's housing, circa 1973, and the total of such units that had been removed from the housing inventory by 1977. In general, this is a phenomenom that has impacted the older rental stock most severely. Nearly one in ten of all the renter occupied units of

EXHIBIT 2

Number of Units in 1973 Structures Removed from Housing Inventory by 1977
(in thousands)

	Total 1973 Units	*Total 1973 Removed by 1977*	*% of 1973 Units Removed by 1977 Total Removed as a % of Total*
Owner Occupied			
1 unit	39,153	488	1.2
2 to 4	2,145	< 70	<2.6
5 or More	555		
Renter Occupied			
1 unit	8,429	578	6.9
2 to 4	6,591	438	6.6
5 to 9	2,770		
10 to 19	2,270	<218	<4.3
20 to 49	1,973		
50 or More	2,172	<168	<4.1

Source: *Annual Housing Survey:* 1973, Series H-150-73A.
                                      1977, Series H-150-77.

1973 that had been constructed in 1939 or earlier had been removed from the inventory by 1977's survey data. And, indeed, there is a linear progression with the most modern of renter occupied units, as would be anticipated, suffering the least degree of attrition. It should be noted, however, that in these groups the attrition level is still far from trivial. Thus, if we were to limit our analysis only to rental units that had been built subsequent to World War II, and by most standards therefore relatively comparable to current construction, we would still have a loss of nearly a half-million renter occupied units.

While some of the most modern of these probably have been shifted to owner occupancy through condominium conversion and the like, there is no question that some of the loss represents stock whose basic parameters were competitive with those currently being constructed, but that may well have been abandoned for reasons other than obsolescence.

In the owner occupied sector there is far more noise, given the relatively low level of incidence of abandonment. Thus, there is some measure of removal shown in the exhibit for relatively recently built, i.e., post-1960 units. Some of this may reflect conversion for alternate uses commercial and otherwise. Still others, however,

EXHIBIT 3

Year Built of Structures Extant in 1973
Yet Removed from the Housing Inventory by 1977
(in thousands)

	Total 1973 Units	Total 1973 Units Removed by 1977	% of 1973 Units Removed by 1977
Owner Occupied			
April 1970 or Later	4,685	182	3.9
1965 to March 1970	6,017	403	3.6
1960 to 1964	5,275	403	3.6
1950 to 1959	9,785	114	1.2
1940 to 1949	4,879	66	1.4
1939 or Earlier	14,013	343	2.4
Renter Occupied			
April 1970 or Later	2,421	19	0.8
1965 to March 1970	3,271	144	3.6
1960 to 1964	2,173	144	3.6
1950 to 1959	3,055	129	4.2
1940 to 1949	2,575	138	5.4
1939 or Earlier	11,189	1,071	9.6

Source: Annual Housing Survey: 1973, Series H-150-73A.
                                   1977, Series H-150-77.

may represent some measure of housing speculation through the purchase and use as rental of condominium units, and sometimes one-family houses as well.

Even allowing for some shifting in categories between ownership and rental and vice versa, and if one were to accept that all of the pre-1939 housing was inadequate (a far from implicit commitment) there still is a significant proportionate and absolute loss of our housing stock that was concentrated in hitherto rental facilities— *and of relatively modern vintage.*

Structure Occupant Characteristics

When analysis is undertaken of household composition of the units occupied in 1973, the dynamics of the situation become somewhat more clarified. If we examine, for example, the rental inventory first, it is clearly the non-"complete" household, (i.e., not two-or-more person household with husband and wife present) that has suffered the most attrition. The greatest level of loss is in other male headed households as well as female headed households.

The situation in housing units occupied by older people is much more complex; the greatest level of attrition is in female headed households and in one-person households as well. The incidence in these two categories is one and a half times that of the two-or-more person household with man and wife present. Yet, within this set, it is the relatively elderly household, those with a head sixty-five years and over that are most positive, with a decline of only 4.2 percent, versus the universe of all renter occupied units that is at the 6.3-percent level (see Exhibit 4).

EXHIBIT 4

**Household Composition by Age of Head of 1973 Housing Units
Removed from the Housing Inventory by 1977
(in thousands)**

	Total 1973 Units	Total 1973 Units Removed by 1977	% of 1973 Units Removed by 1977
Owner Occupied	44,653		
2-or-More Person Households	38,460	1,108	2.5
Male Head, Wife Present,		882	2.3
No Nonrelatives	33,689	743	2.2
65 Years and Over	4,846	74	1.5
Other Male Head	1,633	47	2.9
65 Years and Over	298	2	0.7
Female Head	3,139	93	3.0
65 Years and Over	811	24	3.0
1-Person Households	6,193	226	3.6
65 Years and Over	3,350	120	3.6
Renter Occupied	24,684	1,552	6.3
2-or-More Person Households	16,968	1,013	6.0
Male Head, Wife Present			
No Nonrelatives	11,831	602	5.1
65 Years and Over	1,094	46	4.2
Other Male Head	1,399	115	8.2
65 Years and Over	124	14	11.3
Female Head	3,738	296	7.9
65 Years and Over	366	28	7.7
1-Person Households	7,716	539	7.0
65 Years and Over	2,443	143	5.9

Source: Annual Housing Survey: 1973, Series H-150-73A.
1977, Series H-150-77.

Income

The abandonment of housing units is closely linked with income. Nearly one in ten of all renter occupied units whose tenantry had incomes less than $3,000 in 1973 were removed from the inventory. The same holds true for one in fourteen of the extant inventory in the $3,000 to $6,999 categories. In the highest income categories however, the reduction rate drops dramatically to barely a third of the less fortunate units. The same linkage is clearly mirrored in the owner occupied sector.

Housing of low income individuals is suffering the greatest level of attrition clearly from the materials shown in Exhibit 5. New construction, unless substantially subsidized, may have very little impact on the market that is available for such individuals. As would be guessed, the linkage is most exemplified when the focus is on rent paying capacities.

EXHIBIT 5

Household Income of 1973 Housing Units Removed from the Housing Inventory by 1977

	Total 1973 Units	Total 1973 Units Removed by 1977	% of 1973 Units Removed by 1977
Owner Occupied	44,653	1,108	2.5
Less than - $ 3,000	4,719	214	5.1
$ 3,000 - 4,999	4,262	147	3.4
$ 5,000 - 6,999	3,997	126	3.2
$ 7,000 - 14,999	17,172	458	2.7
$15,000 - 24,999	10,594	112	1.1
$25,000 or More	3,909	26	0.7
Renter Occupied	24,684	1,552	6.3
Less than $ 3,000	4,790	458	9.6
$ 3,000 - 4,999	3,712	280	7.5
$ 5,000 - 6,999	3,477	261	7.5
$ 7,000 - 14,999	9,317	461	4.9
$15,000 - 24,999	2,778	71	2.6
$25,000 or More	611	21	3.4

Source: Annual Housing Survey: 1973, Series H-150-73A.
1977, Series H-150-77.

Rent Levels and the Decline of the Housing Stock

Exhibit 6 indicates the vigorous linkage between rent levels and the disappearance from the housing stock of shelter units. In the four years from 1973 to 1977, fully 15 percent of all the units that rented for less than $79 in the base year were removed from the stock. Moreover, in those same four years, there was a decline of more than a quarter of a million of the physical units that rented from $80 to $90 in the base year.

There was a further attrition, in excess of 400,000 units (6.5 percent of the total) in those rental facilities that rented from a $100 to $149 per month (circa 1973).

Very properly, many of these units should have been removed from the stock, representing far less in the way of amenity than our society has agreed on as the due for any and all of us. But, the gap between new construction costs and the rent dollars required to carry them, and the attrition levels represented here, indicate that to the degree that any of the units could have been saved, the rewards would have been most substantial.

Physically more than a million units, which in 1973 rented for less than $150 a month, literally disappeared from the total housing inventory.

A glance at the General Accounting Office's study on Section 8 indicates that the latter's total level of production in its history, even including future commitment, barely exceeds that figure; and the resulting costs are estimated well in excess of 100-billion dollars.

EXHIBIT 6

**Gross Rents of 1973 Renter-Occupied Units Removed
from the Housing Inventory by 1977
(in thousands)**

	Total 1973 Units	1973 Units Re-moved by 1977	% of 1973 Units Removed by 1977
Total	24,348	1,524	6.3
Less than $79	2,879	431	15.0
$ 80 - 99	2,487	255	10.2
$100 - 149	6,570	424	6.5
$150 - 199	5,366	159	3.0
$200 - 299	2,865	42	1.5
$300 or More	590	21	3.6
Median	$137	$98	3.6

Source: Annual Housing Survey: 1973, Series H-150-73A.
1977, Series H-150-77.

Low rent housing units are literally being removed, and the potential renter, who can only afford low rent, finds the inventory available to him or her shrinking markedly.

The same phenomenom shown in Exhibit 7 exists when we turn to the house values of units removed from the inventory. In general, as would be guessed, these are the very lowest priced of housing. Again, the same admonition must be voiced; many of these should have been removed, but given our new economics is it impossible to halt the pipeline that leads to decline?

EXHIBIT 7

House Value of 1973 Owner Occupied Units Removed from the Housing Inventory by 1977 (in thousands)

	Total 1973 Units	Total 1973 Units Removed by 1977	% of 1973 Units Removed by 1977
Total	35,107	384	1.1
Less than $10,000	3,393	171	5.0
$10,000 - 14,999	4,287	51	1.2
$15,000 - 19,999	5,690	41	0.7
$20,000 - 24,999	5,102	38	0.7
$25,000 - 34,999	8,237	43	0.5
$35,000 - 49,999	5,545	25	0.5
$50,000 and Over	2,854	14	0.5
Median	$24,100	$12,000	

Source: Annual Housing Survey: 1973, Series H-150-73A.
                                           1977, Series H-150-77.

The Urban Impact

The data discussed below have been confined to the lofty levels of the nation and region as a whole. The powerful impact, however, of the movement of housing units out of the inventory upon *specific* local environments should not be underestimated. For this reason, in the material that follows, equivalent data are summarized on two relatively dissimilar metropolitan areas and their central cities: Detroit and Washington.

Exhibit 8 indicates the scale and specific incidence of the removal dynamic from 1974 to 1977 (unfortunately, the data are not available for the 1973 base year earlier used). In the three years under consideration, the Detroit SMSA lost more than 3 percent of its black, owner occupied housing units. This phenomenom was dwarfed

EXHIBIT 8

Occupancy Status by Race of 1974 Housing Units Removed from the Inventory by 1977: Detroit and Washington SMSAs

	DETROIT SMSA			WASHINGTON, D.C. SMSA		
	Total 1974 Units	Total 1974 Units Removed by 1977	% of 1974 Units Removed by 1977	Total 1974 Units	Total 1974 Units Removed by 1977	% of 1974 Units Removed by 1977
Total SMSA						
Owner Occupied	970,300	9,200	0.9	479,000	1,900	0.4
White	828,200	5,000	0.6	393,700	1,100	0.3
Black	137,700	4,200	3.1	79,000	700	0.9
Renter-Occupied	366,300	19,200	5.2	501,900	10,200	2.0
White	247,400	7,500	3.0	322,200	4,800	1.5
Black	115,000	11,700	10.2	167,700	5,200	3.1
Vacant, Year Round	86,200	9,100	10.6	58,400	2,800	4.8
Within Central City						
Owner Occupied	281,200	4,500	1.6	77,700	700	0.9
White	161,000	1,000	0.6	27,400	200	0.7
Black	118,400	3,400	2.9	49,300	500	1.0
Renter Occupied	183,500	13,600	7.4	180,000	6,100	3.4
White	79,300	2,800	3.5	55,800	1,400	2.5
Black	101,900	10,700	10.5	119,900	4,500	3.8
Vacant, Year Round	43,000	8,100	18.8	14,600	1,700	11.6
Outside Central City						
Owner Occupied	689,100	4,700	0.7	401,300	1,200	0.3
White	667,200	4,000	0.6	366,300	900	0.2
Black	19,300	700	3.6	29,700	200	0.7
Renter Occupied	182,800	5,600	3.1	321,900	4,100	1.3
White	168,100	4,600	2.7	266,500	3,400	1.3
Black	13,000	1,000	7.7	47,800	700	1.5
Vacant, Year Round	43,300	900	2.1	43,800	1,100	2.5

Source: *Annual Housing Survey:* 1977, Series H-170-77-5 and H-170-77-18; 1974, Series H-170-74-5 and H-170-74-18.

by the impact on rental facilities. Here the total removal rate was at the 5.2-percent level with an incidence rate of nearly double that, 10.2 percent for black renter occupied units; and this in the space of 3 years. Indeed, the removal rate of vacant year round facilities was over the one in ten mark.

Central Cities

The lower part of the exhibit contrasts the incidence rate within the central city versus the equivalent data for the balance of the SMSA. It is evident from the exhibit that this is far from a solely core city phenomenom. The actual attrition rate for owner occupied units, for example, was similar both in the core and suburban areas. In rental facilities, however, there were fully 13,600 units removed from the central city, and less than half that—5,600—from the balance of the SMSA. Similarly (and indeed even more accentuated), is the imbalance in the removal of vacant year round facilities with nine times as many being removed from the central city—8,100,— to the suburban area's 900.

But, Detroit is thought of as representative merely of the older industrial cities, and indeed one singularly hard hit by population decline and failures of economic function. By way of contrast we have provided equivalent data for Washington, D.C.: both for the SMSA and the central city. Even within this very dynamic market there has been a substantial loss of housing units both in the central city and the suburgan areas as well. In a market in which rentals are at a premium, it is particularly alarming to see the disappearance of no less than 6,100, 1974 units by 1977. And, even the suburban areas have felt the impact of substantial removal from inventory of vacancies with a decline of 1,100—far less than the central city's 1700—but still a very significant number.

In general, as shown in Exhibit 9, once again it is the relatively small scale structures that show the greatest level of attrition, both in the rental and ownership categories.

The impact of this removal of housing, which in 1974 was occupied by low income individuals, is illustrated in Exhibit 10. While it is far from an exclusively low income phenomenom, the linkage is most evident. In three years, 3.5 percent of all the units owned by individuals with incomes of less than $3,000 a year had disappeared from the housing stock in Detroit.

The pattern is even more clear cut when focused on renters as in Exhibit 11. More than one in nine of the units occupied by individuals with incomes less than $3,000, one in eleven occupied by those at the $3,000—$4,999 level, and more than one in fifteen at those from the $5,000 to $10,000 levels had been removed from the stock.

The linkage, though less deep, is followed precisely in Washington, D.C.. The incidence rate may be half as great; the impact; however, on housing for relatively low income individuals is equally vivid.

Finally, in Exhibits 12 and 13, data are presented on gross rents as of 1974 as well as house values for the same dates. As would be guessed, these closely parallel the findings by income. Housing costs are going up not only because of inflation in the rents and values of extant housing but even more strikingly because of the removal from the inventory of the less expensive housing stock.

Summary and Conclusions

America, and most specifically its central cities, are losing housing that cannot be replicated without massive subsidies. Some of the scrappage rate undoubtedly impacts units that are no longer admissible to present day housing standards. And, to this degree, the phenomenom is a tribute to the sheer vitality of America's housing markets. But, some of it unquestionably represents units whose utility is far less questionable and whose replacement is enormously expensive. As substantial rehabilitation costs under Section 8 soar to the $50,000 a unit figure, as the rent subsidy required for new construction in some areas is at the $10,000 a year mark, the importance of preserving the preservable, of making sure that the long pipeline which ultimately results in abandonment is interrupted through appropriate maintenance conditions must become front and center in public understanding—and public action as well.

EXHIBIT 9

Number of Units in 1974 Structures Removed from the Housing Inventory by 1977: Detroit and Washington SMSAs (occupied units only)

	DETROIT SMSA			WASHINGTON, D.C. SMSA		
	Total 1974 Units	Total 1974 Units Removed by 1977	% of 1974 Units Removed by 1977	Total 1974 Units	Total 1974 Units Removed by 1977	% of 1974 Units Removed by 1977
Total SMSA						
Owner Occupied	970,300	9,200	0.9	479,000	1,900	0.4
1 unit	907,000	8,300	0.9	456,400	1,500	0.3
2 to 4	39,800	800	2.0	4,300	100	2.3
5 or more	8,500	—	—	14,900	200	1.3
Mobile home or trailer	—	—	—	—	—	—
Renter Occupied	366,300	19,200	5.2	501,900	10,200	2.0
1 unit	111,900	5,600	5.0	103,200	2,000	1.9
2 to 4	102,200	5,400	5.3	56,200	2,600	4.6
5 to 9	51,700	1,900	3.7	70,400	1,100	1.6
10 to 19	33,100	1,800	5.4	133,400	1,100	0.8
20 to 49	32,800	2,400	7.3	27,900	400	1.4
50 or more	32,300	2,200	6.8	110,400	300	0.3
Mobile home or trailer	—	—	—	—	—	—
Within Central City						
Owner Occupied	281,200	4,500	1.6	77,700	700	0.9
1 unit	249,900	3,800	1.5	70,000	600	0.9
2 to 4	28,200	700	2.5	1,700	100	5.9
5 or more	2,900	—	—	6,000	—	—
Mobile home or trailer	—	—	—	—	—	—
Renter Occupied	183,500	13,600	7.4	180,000	6,100	3.4
1 unit	51,400	3,500	6.8	29,000	1,300	4.5
2 to 4	62,400	4,100	6.6	31,200	1,700	5.4
5 to 9	12,900	1,100	8.5	20,500	1,000	4.9
10 to 19	14,200	1,100	7.7	32,200	600	1.9
20 to 49	22,400	1,700	7.6	16,200	400	2.5
50 or more	20,200	2,000	10.6	51,000	1,000	2.0
Mobile home or trailer	—	—	—	—	—	—

EXHIBIT 9 (Continued)

	DETROIT SMSA			WASHINGTON, D.C. SMSA		
	Total 1974 Units	Total 1974 Units Removed by 1977	% of 1974 Units Removed by 1977	Total 1974 Units	Total 1974 Units Removed by 1977	% of 1974 Units Removed by 1977
Outside Central City						
Owner Occupied						
1 unit	689,000	4,700	0.7	401,300	1,200	0.3
2 to 4	657,100	4,600	0.7	386,400	900	0.2
5 or more	11,600	100	0.9	2,700	—	—
Mobilie home or trailer	5,600	—	—	8,900	200	2.2
Renter Occupied	—			—	—	—
1 unit	182,800	5,600	3.1	321,900	4,100	1.3
2 to 4	60,500	2,100	3.5	74,200	700	0.9
5 to 9	39,800	1,300	3.3	25,000	900	3.6
10 to 19	38,900	800	2.1	49,800	100	0.2
20 to 49	18,900	700	3.7	101,200	500	0.5
50 or more	10,400	600	5.8	11,700	—	—
Mobile home or trailer	12,100	200	1.7	59,400	1,900	3.2

Source: U.S. Bureau of the Census. *Annual Housing Survey: 1977, Housing Characteristics for Selected Metropolitan Areas,* Series H-170-77-5 and H-170-77-18, 1980.

Annual Housing Survey: 1977, Series H-170-77-5 and H-170-77-18.
1974, Series H-170-74-5 and H-170-74-18.

EXHIBIT 10

Annual Incomes of Households in 1974 Structures Removed from the Housing Inventory by 1977: Detroit and Washington SMSAs (owner occupied only)

	DETROIT SMSA				WASHINGTON, D.C. SMSA	
	Total 1974 Units	Total 1974 Units Removed by 1977	% of 1974 Units Removed by 1977	Total 1974 Units	Total 1974 Units Removed by 1977	% of 1974 Units Removed by 1977
Total SMSA	970,300	9,200	0.9	479,000	1,900	4.0
Less than $ 3,000	56,300	1,000	1.8	13,100	200	1.5
$ 3,000- 4,999	59,100	1,000	1.7	11,900	100	0.8
$ 5,000- 6,999	59,100	900	1.5	14,000	200	1.4
$ 7,000- 9,999	87,500	700	0.8	24,200	—	—
$10,000- 14,999	200,400	3,000	1.5	65,800	500	0.8
$15,000- 24,999	338,300	2,200	0.7	165,800	300	0.2
$25,000 or More	169,500	200	0.1	184,300	400	0.2
Within Central City	281,200	4,500	1.6	77,700	700	0.9
Less than $ 3,000	26,000	900	3.5	4,500	100	2.2
$ 3,000- 4,999	29,700	500	1.7	4,000	—	—
$ 5,000- 6,999	26,600	900	3.4	5,300	100	1.9
$ 7,000- 9,999	37,500	400	1.1	7,200	—	2.0
$10,000- 14,999	59,200	800	1.4	14,700	300	0.9
$15,000- 24,999	75,300	700	0.9	21,800	200	0.1
$25,000 or More	27,000	100	0.4	20,000	—	—
Outside Central City	689,100	4,700	0.7	301,200	1,200	0.2
Less than $ 3,000	30,400	200	1.0	8,400	100	1.1
$ 3,000- 4,999	29,400	400	2.3	7,800	100	1.2
$ 5,000- 6,999	32,500	—	—	8,700	100	1.1
$ 7,000- 9,999	50,000	300	1.1	16,800	—	—
$10,000- 14,999	141,300	2,200	1.6	41,100	200	4.0
$15,000- 24,999	263,000	1,400	0.5	133,000	100	0.1
$25,000 or More	142,400	200	0.1	153,200	400	0.2

Source: Annual Housing Survey: 1977, Series H-170-77-5 and H-170-77-18; 1974, Series H-170-74-5 and H-170-74-18.

EXHIBIT 11

Annual Incomes of Households in 1974 Structures Removed from the Housing Inventory by 1977: Detroit and Washington SMSAs (renter occupied only)

	DETROIT SMSA			WASHINGTON, D.C. SMSA		
	Total 1974 Units	Total 1974 Units Removed by 1977	% of 1974 Units Removed by 1977	Total 1974 Units	Total 1974 Units Removed by 1977	% of 1974 Units Removed by 1977
Total SMSA	366,300	19,200	5.2	501,900	10,200	2.0
Less than $ 3,000	64,900	7,000	10.8	39,000	1,500	3.8
$ 3,000- 4,999	50,300	4,200	8.3	41,100	2,900	7.1
$ 5,000- 6,999	37,600	2,200	5.9	48,500	1,800	3.7
$ 7,000- 9,999	55,300	2,200	4.0	86,900	1,900	2.2
$10,000- 14,999	81,200	2,300	2.8	128,400	1,100	0.9
$15,000- 24,999	57,800	1,300	2.2	115,100	900	0.8
$25,000 or More	19,000	—	—	43,000	100	0.2
Within Central City	183,500	3,600	2.0	180,000	6,100	3.4
Less than $ 3,000	46,200	5,300	11.5	22,200	1,100	5.0
$ 3,000- 4,999	32,600	2,900	8.9	20,900	900	4.3
$ 5,000- 6,999	21,700	1,500	6.9	23,300	1,100	4.7
$ 7,000- 9,999	28,900	2,100	7.3	35,500	1,400	3.9
$10,000- 14,999	30,700	1,100	3.6	39,400	900	2.3
$15,000- 24,999	18,800	500	2.7	28,500	600	2.1
$25,000 or More	4,500	—	—	10,300	100	1.0
Outside Central City	182,800	5,600	3.1	321,900	4,100	1.3
Less than $ 3,000	18,700	1,600	8.6	16,800	400	2.4
$ 3,000- 4,999	17,600	1,300	7.4	20,300	2,000	9.9
$ 5,000- 6,999	15,900	600	3.8	25,200	700	2.8
$ 7,000- 9,999	26,400	200	0.8	51,400	500	1.0
$10,000- 14,999	50,400	1,100	2.2	89,000	200	0.2
$15,000- 24,999	39,000	800	2.1	86,600	200	0.2
$25,000 or More	14,700	—	—	32,700	200	0.6

Source: Annual Housing Survey, 1974, Series H-170-74-5 and H-170-74-18; 1977, Series H-170-77-5 and H-170-77-18.

EXHIBIT 12

Gross Rents of 1974 Renter-Occupied Units Removed from Housing Inventory by 1977: Detroit and Washington SMSAs

	DETROIT SMSA			WASHINGTON, D.C. SMSA		
	Total 1974 Units	Total 1974 Units Removed by 1977	% of 1974 Units Removed by 1977	Total 1974 Units	Total 1974 Units Removed by 1977	% of 1974 Units Removed by 1977
Total SMSA						
Less than $ 79	27,000	3,000	11.1	16,500	1,300	7.9
$ 80 - 99	33,000	3,700	11.0	12,400	1,400	11.3
$100 - 149	104,600	8,000	7.6	103,500	3,700	3.6
$150 - 199	101,400	2,700	2.7	145,600	1,800	1.2
$200 - 299	75,800	800	1.1	159,800	800	0.5
$300 or more	12,000	—	—	51,000	400	0.8
Median	$156	$114	73.08	$189	$118	62.4
Within Central City						
Less than $ 79	21,600	2,300	10.6	12,500	600	4.8
$ 80 - 99	25,700	2,800	10.9	9,500	900	9.5
$100 - 149	76,800	6,100	7.9	65,800	1,800	2.7
$150 - 199	42,000	1,700	4.0	49,800	1,200	2.4
$200 - 299	11,200	200	1.8	30,000	700	2.3
$300 or more	1,300	—	—	10,100	300	3.0
Median	$126	$109	86.5	$151	$126	83.4
Outside Central City						
Less than $ 79	5,300	600	11.3	4,100	600	14.6
$ 80 - 99	8,100	1,000	12.3	2,900	500	17.2
$100 - 149	27,700	1,800	6.5	36,700	1,800	4.9
$150 - 199	59,500	1,000	1.7	95,800	600	0.6
$200 - 299	64,700	600	0.9	129,800	100	0.08
$300 or more	10,600	—	—	41,000	100	0.2
Median	$189	$134	70.9	$212	$112	52.8

Source: Annual Housing Survey, 1974, Series H-170-74-5 and H-170-74-18; 1977, Series H-170-77-5 and H-170-77-18.

EXHIBIT 13

House Values of 1974 Owner-Occupied Units Removed from Housing Inventory by 1977: Detroit and Washington SMSAs

	DETROIT SMSA			WASHINGTON, D.C. SMSA		
	Total 1974 Units	Total 1974 Units Removed by 1977	% of 1974 Units Removed by 1977	Total 1974 Units	Total 1974 Units Removed by 1977	% of 1974 Units Removed by 1977
Total SMSA						
Less than $10,000	19,200	6,100	31.8	1,000	—	—
$10,000- 14,999	55,900	1,400	2.5	1,600	—	—
$15,000- 19,999	142,100	2,000	1.4	9,500	—	—
$20,000- 24,999	174,100	1,200	0.7	17,400	—	—
$25,000- 34,999	262,000	400	0.2	57,000	300	0.5
$35,000- 49,999	142,600	800	0.6	141,900	400	0.3
$50,000 and over	85,400	300	0.4	213,800	200	0.1
Median	$26,900	$14,200	52.8	$49,200	—	—
Within Central City						
Less than $10,000	14,600	900	6.2	200	—	—
$10,000- 14,999	42,800	1,500	3.5	1,300	—	—
$15,000- 19,999	84,000	900	1.1	6,900	—	—
$20,000- 24,999	64,300	300	0.5	9,800	—	—
$25,000- 34,999	38,600	—	—	20,100	100	0.5
$35,000- 49,999	5,300	—	—	12,800	200	1.6
$50,000 and over	1,300	—	—	17,100	—	—
Median	$19,000	$13,000	68.4	$32,900	—	—
Outside Central City						
Less than $10,000	4,700	500	10.6	700	—	—
$10,000- 14,999	13,200	500	3.8	300	—	—
$15,000- 19,999	58,100	300	0.5	2,600	—	—
$20,000- 24,999	109,800	200	0.2	7,700	—	—
$25,000- 34,999	226,400	800	0.4	36,900	200	0.5
$35,000- 49,999	137,400	—	—	129,100	100	0.1
$50,000 and over	84,100	300	0.4	196,700	200	0.1
Median	$30,800	—	—	$50,000+	—	—

Source: *Annual Housing Survey,* 1974, Series H-170-74-5 and H-170-74-18; 1977, Series H-170-77-5 and H-170-77-18.

Appendix B
Summary of Findings
The Conversion of Rental Housing to Condominiums and Cooperatives*

Summary

The recent growth of condominium and cooperative conversions is a response to basic changes in the nation's social and housing market conditions that, in its course, helps some and hurts others. For this reason, conversion has sparked considerable controversy— a controversy exacerbated by the shortage of information about what is taking place. This report, prepared in response to a Congressional directive, presents the results of a multifaceted study designed to provide this information. It documents the present and probable future extent and location of conversions, the factors contributing to their increasing numbers, and their effects—on people, neighborhoods, and communities. As will be apparent, the scope, causes, and consequences of the conversion phenomenon are, in many ways, quite different than is generally understood.

*Prepared by U.S. Department of Housing and Urban Development, Office of Policy Development and Research, Division of Policy Studies. (Washington, D.C.; U.S. Government Printing Office, June, 1980).

Conversion changes the legal form of a multifamily rental property from single ownership by a landlord to multiple ownership. In most condominium conversions, the landlord first sells the property to a developer specializing in conversion who then sells the individual units. Most conversions are accompanied by some minor or cosmetic improvements to the property's condition, equipment, or amenities; however, a few conversions have involved the substantial rehabilitation of older buildings.

Up to now, the number of conversions that have taken place in the nation has generally not been known because of the difficulty of assembling information from local public records, because the processes that govern conversions in various housing markets differ, and because of differences in terminology regarding conversions across these markets. Having a common definition that applies across jurisdictions is a prerequisite for arriving at a national count and analyzing the significance of the volume of conversion activity. For the purposes of this study, a rental building is considered to be converted to condominium ownership when the first unit is sold as a condominium. In New York, where most of the nation's cooperative conversions occur, a rental building is considered to be converted to a cooperative when the legally required number of tenants have purchased shares.

Very few rental properties were converted to multiple ownership in this country prior to 1970. Since then, 366,000 rental housing units have been converted. Of these, only 18,000 are cooperative conversions. The rate of conversion has been accelerating: in the period 1977 through 1979, 260,000 units were converted, 71 percent of the decade's total. To date, conversion activity has been concentrated in larger metropolitan areas: 76 percent of all conversions have occurred in the thirty-seven largest SMSAs, and 59 percent have taken place in just twelve of these areas. There is some evidence, however, that the conversion phenomenon may be expanding to or increasing in smaller metropolitan areas.

Within the largest metropolitan areas of the nation, a surprisingly large amount of conversion (49 percent) has occurred in suburban jurisdictions; the remaining 51 percent has taken place within central cities.

By the end of 1979, 1.3 percent of the nation's occupied rental housing stock had been converted. However, there is considerable variation from one metropolitan area to another, as well as within each area. For example, in the New York City and Los Angeles areas, 1 percent of all rental units were converted during the 1970s, compared to 6 percent or more in the Chicago, Denver, and Washington, D.C. areas. There are some atypical suburban communities and smaller cities where as much as 20 to 30 percent of the rental stock has been converted, and a few sections of cities where more than 30 percent of the rental stock has been converted.

Nationally, the volume of condominium and cooperative conversion activity is expected to increase through 1985. The analysis suggests that the number of conversions will increase each year, but at successively decreasing rates. A trend-line projection of conversion volumes through the year 1985, based on past experience, but modified to consider supply, demand, and current financial market factors, suggests that about 1.1-million rental units will be converted during this six-year period. Of course, future conversion volumes may be influenced by many currently unknown factors, including long-term financial conditions, government regulation, or any changes that may be made to the Federal tax code.

There are a few metropolitan areas where the supply of rental properties most suited to conversion (using market derived standards that have applied to date) will be nearly exhausted within five years.

Conversions have been more numerous in metropolitan areas characterized by strong and growing market demand for home-ownership. Conversions are not, as some market specialists believe, associated with distressed rental markets. For example, there is no evidence that conversions are concentrated in metropolitan areas with higher than average rental vacancy rates or depressed rent levels. Furthermore, legislated rent controls are not necessary conditions for or leading causes of conversions, if for no other reason than that so few of the jurisdictions with conversions have enacted such measures.

In most parts of the country, however, average operating margins for rental properties do appear to be declining. This has contributed to apartment owners' willingness to sell their buildings to converters. For many rental property owners, no projected amount of rental income, allowable tax depreciation, property appreciation, or tax sheltering can equal the return received on the sale of their properties for conversion. Strong demand for the kinds of housing represented by condominiums and cooperatives, combined with potentially large profits, has made converters willing to pay prices for rental properties that are far in excess of what these buildings could command based on continued use as rentals. The ability of converters, then, to turn over individual units in these buildings for higher prices is, in great measure, a function of increasing demand for home-ownership that is fueled by rising incomes and inflation. Recent inflation also tends to shift the homebuying demand of an increasing number of middle income households from traditional single-family houses, that may be priced too high, to less expensive condominiums and cooperatives.

The number of conversions tends to be somewhat greater in metropolitan areas that are characterized by growing household populations and larger proportions of households having one or two persons, or headed by an individual thirty-five-years old or less. Conversions are also somewhat more numerous in areas where more households have incomes above $25,000, where luxury buildings form a higher proportion of the rental stock, and where the rental housing stock is relatively new.

Conversions are products of a shift in housing demand, and a corresponding shift in the use of the existing housing supply away from rental toward ownership. The net effect of conversions on the balance of supply and demand can be estimated by considering the pre- and post-conversion tenure status of households affected by conversion. Those renters who buy contribute to a reduction of overall renter demand; many converted units remain available as rentals; and some tenants move out upon conversion and purchase a unit elsewhere. The cumulative effect of these factors contributes to a significant moderation of the actual supply impact on the rental market. This analysis indicates, nationally, that for every 100-rental units converted, there is a *net* increase of 5 units for sale to owners, and a *net* decrease of 5 available rental units. In other words, when changes in demand and supply resulting from conversion are juxtaposed, the effect on the rental market is considerably less than the total of all units converted.

Based on these figures and the volume of conversions nationally, the net effect of conversions on the rental market has been to reduce the nation's supply of available rentals by 18,000 units in the 1970 to 1979 period.

The impact of conversions can also be assessed in relation to other components of change in the rental housing market. Considering total demand for rental housing, the amount of new rental housing being produced, and losses to the rental inventory through various means, there has been a shortfall of rental housing in the last several years. Conversions have contributed to this shortfall. For example, in 1977, they accounted for 17 percent of excess demand over supply. Unlike other losses of rental housing, however, conversion often results in a concomitant reduction in renter demand because previous renters become homeowners.

Conversion can produce either very substantial or minimal movement of households in and out of converting buildings, depending on the proportion of prior tenants who either buy converted units or remain in the buildings as renters. Of all households occupying units in buildings that were converted after January 1977, 58 percent had moved out as of January 1980. The remaining 42 percent continued to live in the buildings as either owners (22 percent) or renters (20 percent) along with new occupants who had moved in since the conversion; most of the new occupants (41 percent of all current residents) owned their units but the remainder (17 percent) rented. Consequently, the residents of these buildings after conversion were 63 percent owner occupants and 37 percent renters.

Of the 37 percent of post-conversion residents who rent their units, about one-half currently lease from the converter/developer, and one-half from investors or relatives. That there are households renting from converter/developers reflects the fact that some recently converted buildings are still in the transition process: a portion of these renters are finishing out current leases; and a portion are continuing to rent, as permitted by local law. Some of these units may also be held as long-term investments by the converter.

Thirty-nine percent of converted units are bought by households earning more than $30,000 annually; but, since converted rental units are often less expensive than newly constructed condominiums and cooperatives or single-family homes, they also provide a new avenue of ownership for smaller, younger households who have incomes insufficient to buy other types of housing.

Nearly two-thirds of the owner occupant households in converted buildings are headed by an individual who holds a professional or managerial position; about one-half are thirty-five or younger, while only one-fifth are over fifty-five, and only 9 percent are over sixty-five. About 10 percent of the owner occupiers of converted units are black, whereas only 7 percent of all owner occupants in the nation are black.

Fifty-seven percent of the owner occupant households in converted buildings are single persons (36 percent single women and 21 percent single men) compared to merely 14 percent (10 percent women and 4 percent men) of all owner occupants in the nation.

Compared to all owner occupants nationally, fewer owner occupants of converted buildings are elderly (9 percent versus 22 percent). When buyers who previously rented in the converted buildings are compared with buyers coming from outside, the former tend to be older and to have higher incomes.

Two-thirds of all owner occupants name economic factors as their primary reasons for buying: to gain a hedge against inflation; to stabilize housing costs; to provide a tax shelter or investment; to find an alternative to singe-family housing; or to obtain a buyer discount. Tenant buyers are more likely than outside buyers to say they bought because they liked the location and did not want to move.

Most of those who buy converted units increase their expenditure for housing. Total monthly outlays made by tenant buyers are typically 36-percent higher than what they paid in rent, while the median increase in monthly housing costs for buyers coming from other housing is 62 percent; however, these figures do not take into account tax benefits associated with owning a home or potential appreciation.

Those who do not buy, but either move from converting buildings or remain there as renters come from all age and income categories. Renters in converted units tend to have lower incomes than owners in the same buildings; but incomes that are much higher than all renters nationally. While 39 percent of converted unit owners earn over $30,000 annually, only 22 percent of renters have this level of income.

Tenants of converting buildings typically are given about seventy days by the converter to decide whether or not to buy. Many tenants are distressed—at least initially—by the prospect of conversion. About one-fourth of tenants who bought or continued to rent their units after conversion report that they felt under pressure to buy; the pressure was not so much caused by harassment or high pressured sales tactics as it was by being faced with an unanticipated housing decision. However, nearly three-fourths of those who move from converting buildings (former residents) say that they felt under pressure, more than likely caused by the disruption and uncertainties associated with such a move. More elderly than nonelderly tenants (28 percent versus 18 percent) felt pressured by the conversion experience.

One-half of all former residents of converted buildings had some difficulty in finding new housing; elderly, nonwhite, and lower income former tenants are more likely to report such difficulty.

One of the major concerns relating to conversion is the extent to which it involuntarily displaces prior tenants. Including both those who had moved out as of January 1980 (58 percent) and those who continue to rent but may yet move (an estimated 8 percent), the average proportion of prior tenants who move out following conversion may be as high as two-thirds. However, not all of these moves will be involuntary; nationally, nearly 40 percent of all renters move at least once each year.

If displacement is defined as movement to rental housing that is of similar or lower quality at higher cost, or of lower quality at equivalent cost, then 18 percent of all households (27 percent of households with persons age sixty and over) who moved from converting buildings have experienced the adverse effects of displacement; this is equal to 10 percent of those who resided in converted buildings prior to conversion. Another 6 percent of all former residents moved to lower quality housing renting for less than they had paid prior to conversion.

Some conversions require people with low or moderate incomes to move because they cannot afford to buy their apartments. About 42 percent of those who moved out of converted buildings had incomes that, according to generally accepted criteria, were too low to have permitted them to buy their converted units; 47 percent of all former residents say they did not purchase because they believed they could not afford to do so.

Seventy percent of all former residents continue to rent after conversion, and they typically experience rent increases of less than 10 percent; however, 28 percent pay at least 25-percent more for rent. Those former residents who decide to buy housing elsewhere typically pay 68-percent more per month for housing, without taking into account possible tax savings and appreciation. Less than one-fifth of all former residents consider their new residence to be inferior to the one they lived in prior to conversion.

Ninety percent of all former residents indicate they are satisfied with their new housing; this is roughly the same degree of housing satisfaction reported for those replacing them in the converted buildings. Nearly three-fourths of all former residents have moved to a new neighborhood as good as or better than their old one. Eighty percent live as close or closer to friends and relatives as before the move. Those with lower incomes, however, are more likely to report that their neighborhood is worse than the old one.

Forty-three percent of all former residents are under age thirty-six and one-fifth are over sixty-five.

Those who move have incomes that are, on average, lower (20 percent under $12,500) than buyers of converted units (12 percent under $12,500), but higher than renters in converted buildings. About 12 percent of all those who move from converted buildings are elderly households with incomes of less than $12,500. Eleven percent are black; one percent are Hispanic.

Conversions, when sufficiently numerous and concentrated, can have significant impacts not only on individual households but also on entire communities or neighborhoods. Reassessment of property following conversion leads to increased revenue from local property taxes. The degree of impact is a function of the particular jurisdiction's tax rates for various classes of property, its assessment practices, and provisions providing tax relief for special classes of property owners. When weighed against the total revenue from property taxes, however, the total impact of conversions to date on local property tax revenues has been very small. Less clear is the impact that conversions may have, in neighborhoods where concentrated, on demands for public services and, therefore, on the long term pattern of public expenditures. Available evidence, however, suggests that the demand for public services in these neighborhoods is basically unaffected by conversions.

It is useful to classify conversions as occurring in one of three types of neighborhood: central city nonrevitalizing, central city revitalizing, and suburban nonrevitalizing. In almost two-thirds of the central cities located in the thirty-seven largest metropolitan areas, conversions are concentrated in nonrevitalizing neighborhoods characterized by above average median incomes, rent levels, and housing values, and by rental vacancy rates equal to or below the city average. One-third of the central cities had conversion activity in at least one revitalizing neighborhood. However, these same cities had a majority of their conversion activity in nonrevitalizing neighborhoods. Conversion has tended to lag behind rather than serve as a catalyst for other reinvestment in revitalizing areas. Conversion activity has had little impact on housing conditions in either type of central city neighborhood; however, as indicated earlier, some converting buildings in revitalizing neighborhoods do undergo major rehabilitation.

In neither type of central city neighborhood has conversion activity produced very much change in the socioeconomic characteristics of residents. In central city revitalizing neighborhoods, however, socioeconomic changes appear to result from the overall revitalization process, not necessarily from conversion; significant population changes had occurred in these neighborhoods prior to the onset of conversions. In central cities, pre- and post-conversion residents are similar in most respects.

However, post-conversion residents are slightly less likely to be nonwhite (15 percent versus 21 percent before conversion), over age sixty-five (17 percent versus 23 percent), or retired (17 percent versus 23 percent), and more likely to be employed in professional or managerial jobs (63 percent versus 59 percent). Just over one-fourth (27 percent) of those moving to converted buildings in central cities lived in the same neighborhood prior to the move, 34 percent lived in another city neighorhood, 12 percent lived in one of the city's suburbs, and the balance (27 percent) came from another city.

Conversion has occurred in nonrevitalizing suburban locations in twenty-siven of the thirty-seven largest metropolitan areas; nineteen such areas have higher proportions of their total conversion activity in suburbs than in their central cities. These are nearly always close in, economically stable suburbs, whose residents are typically middle to upper-middle-income whites. More of the conversions here involve garden and townhouse style rather than high rise apartments. These conversions have had a negligible impact on housing quality, since most involve minor repairs to properties already in sound condition.

Pre- and post-conversion residents of these buildings are similar, although post-conversion households are slightly more likely to be nonwhite (17 percent versus 12 percent before conversion) and to hold professional or managerial positions (59 percent versus fifty-two percent) and less likely to earn incomes below $12,500 (sixteen percent versus twenty-seven percent), to be retired (eleven percent versus twenty-one percent), or to be over age sixty-five (thirteen percent versus eighteen percent). Less than one-fourth of the post-conversion residents of these buildings come from other housing in the same neighborhoods.

Federal government programs have so far played minor roles in relation to condominium and cooperative conversions. Programs of secondary mortgage market insitutions (the Federal National Mortgage Association and the Federal Home Loan Mortgage Corporation) make it easier to finance and resell converted units that meet their criteria for purchase; thus, FNMA and FHLMC indirectly influence such practices as the proportion of presales, proportion of units occupied by owners, and condition of properties. A few state and local governments, many with financial support from the Federal government, have developed innovative programs intended to provide technical and financial assistance to groups seeking to convert their buildings, to subsidize low- and moderate-income households in converted buildings, or to assist households relocating after conversion.

State and local governments also have begun to respond to conversions with various types of regulatory legislation. Conversion related regulations can be categorized as follows: those designed to protect tenants of converting buildings; those intended to protect buyers of converted units; those developed to preserve the supply of rental housing; and those aimed at preserving the supply of low- to moderate-income housing. To date, very few states and localities have passed the latter two types of legislation.

Just under one-half of the states have legislated protections for tenants of converting buildings; and, about one-half have laws protecting purchasers of both new and converted condominium units. States that have enacted tenant or buyer protection measures often contain metropolitan areas that are experiencing high levels of conversion.

At the local level, although just over one-third of all jurisdictions have had or still have conversion activity, fewer than one in five of those experiencing conversions has passed a regulatory ordinance. Larger jurisdictions and those with more conversions are more likely to adopt such legislation. About 6 percent of jurisdictions with past or present conversions have at one time or another adopted temporary moratoria halting all conversion activity.

Nearly all local regulatory ordinances provide some protections to tenants in converting buildings. Such ordinances typically require 90 to 180 days notice to tenants of a planned conversion. A few localities offer special protections to elderly and handicapped tenants, such as the right to extend their lease period.

Most ordinances protect condominium buyers by requiring code inspection, engineering reports, and disclosure statements, or warranties on major structural features. A few ordinances seek to preserve the local rental stock, typically by restricting conversions when the rental vacancy rate drops below a certain percentage.

With regard to government action to affect the level of conversion activity, three of every four local chief executives prefer that neither the state nor federal government act either to encourage or to discourage conversions. Over 60 percent also believe that local governments should avoid such actions. Of those who do see a role for government, a somewhat larger proportion prefers actions that would encourage rather than discourage conversions, such as programs to enable low- and moderate-income households to purchase their units or technical assistance programs for tenant sponsored conversions.

Officials representing jurisdictions with heavy recent conversion activity are more likely than others to favor government regulatory intervention. About one-fifth of these would have any level of government act to discourage conversions. Similar proportions of this group would have local or state governments act to encourage conversions. Nevertheless, majorities of those local officials with the most conversion experience prefer that the state and federal governments neither encourage nor discourage conversions.

Future changes in the volume, location, and character of conversions could, of course, alter the impacts that have been specified here—both positive and negative—on people, neighborhoods, and communities. For instance, if there is a homeownership market for units that are older or of lower quality than those currently being converted, a larger proportion of future conversions may involve rehabilitation and revitalization. This would result in more dramatic changes in the housing stock than has presently been observed. On the other hand, if such buildings contain higher proportions of elderly, minority, or low-income residents, the frequency with which conversion creates hardship for such households may also increase.

Bibliography

Aberle, John W., and Wang, Pe Sheng. *The Characteristics, Preferences, and Home Buying, Intentions of Apartment Residents in San Jose, Cal.* San Jose State College: School of Business Administration, 1965.

Abt Associates, Inc. *Administrative Agency Experiment Evaluation. Experimental Housing Allowance Program* (Annual Report). Springfield, Vir.: NTIS, (Annual).

Abt Associates, Inc. *Agency Program Manual of the Administrative Agency. Experiment of the Experimental Housing Allowance Program.* Springfield, Vir.: NTIS, 1974.

American Society of Planning Officials. *Apartments in the Suburbs.* Chicago, Ill: June 1964.

Anderson, Kenneth; Petty, Carol Bender; and Anderson, Karen. *Income/Expense Analysis: Apartments. 1979 Edition.* Chicago, Ill.: Institute of Real Estate Management, 1979.

Anderson, Kenneth; Petty, Carol Bender; and Pawlarczyk, Sharon. *Income/Expense Analysis: Apartments. 1978 Edition.* Chicago, Ill.: Institute of Real Estate Management, 1978.

"Apartments in Suburbia: Local Responsibility and Judicial Restraint." *Northwestern University Law Review,* July/August 1964, pp. 344-432.

Arnault, E. Jane. "Optimal Maintenance Under Rent Control with Quality Constraints." *American Real Estate and Urban Economics Association Journal,* Summer 1975.

Atlas, John, and Dreier, Peter. "The Housing crisis and the tenant's revolt." *Social Policy,* Jan/Feb. 1980, p. 13-24.

Babcock, Richard F., and Bosselman, Fred P. "Suburban Zoning and the Apartment Boom." *University of Pennsylvania Law Review,* June 1963, pp. 1040-191.

Barnett, Lance, C. *How Housing Allowances Affect Housing Prices. Housing Assistance Supply Experiment.* Santa Monica, Calif. Rand Corp., 1979.

Barnett, Lance C. *Using Hedonic Indexes to Measure Housing Quality: Housing Assistance Supply Experiment.* Santa Monica, Calif.: Rand Corp., 1979.

Bashin, Sheldon L. *Evaluation of Proposed Shallow Subsidy Rental Housing Production Program.* Springfield, Vir.: NTLS, 1973.

Battelle Memorial Institute. *Study and Evaluation of Integrating the Handicapped in HUD Housing.* Columbus, Ohio: The Institute, 1977.

Bell, Felicia L. *Analysis of Displacement Caused by Condominium Conversion.* Washington, D.C.: D.C. Department of Housing and Community Development, 1979.

Black, J. Thomas. *Prospects for Rental Housing Production Under Rent Control: A case Study of Washington, D.C.* Washington, D.C.: Urban Land Instutute, 1976.

Boston Urban Observatory. *Subsidized Multi-family Rental Housing in the Boston Metropolitan Area.* Springfield, Vir.: NTIS, 1973.

Bourdon, Richard. *Condominium Conversions: Possible Changes in Federal Tax Laws to Discourage Conversions and Assist Rental Housing.* Washington, D.C.: Library of Congress, Congressional Research Service, 1980.

Brueggeman, William B. *Tax Reform. Tax Incentives and Investment Returns On Rental Housing.* Springfield, Vir.: NTIS, 1977.

Buck, Rinker, "The City's Biggest Landlord." *New York,* 10 September 1979, p. 50-58.

Burchell, Robert W. *Planned Unit Development: New Communities American Style.* New Brunswick, N.J.: Center for Urban Policy Research, 1972.

California State Office of Planning and Research. *Condos Co-ops, and Conversions: A Guide to Rental Conversions for Local Officials.* Washington, D.C.: U.S. Department of Housing and Urban Development, 1979.

Cherry, R., and Ford, E.J., Jr. "Concentrated of Rental Housing Property and Rental Housing Markets in Urban Areas." *American Real Estate and Urban Economics Association Journal,* Spring 1975, p. 7-16.

Coalition to Save New York. *A Policy Review of Rental Housing in New York City.* (Prepared by Real Estate Research Corporation). New York, April 1975.

Conchado, Sandra N., and Nolan, William P. "Building Abandonment in New York City." *New York Law Forum* 16, no. 4 (1970): 798-862.

Corcoran, Joseph E. "King's Lynne: Public Housing Becomes Private Housing." *Urban Land,* March 1980, p. 6-12.

Davidson, Harold A. "The Impact of Rent Control on Apartment Investment." *Appraisal Journal,* October 1978, p. 570-80.

DeLeeuw, Frank. *The Section 23 Leasing Program.* Washington, D.C.: Urban Institute, 1973.

DeLeeuw, F., and Ekanem, N. *Time Lags in the Rental Housing Market.* Springfield, Vir.: NTIS, 1970.

Denver Planning Office. *Apartment Growth in Denver: A Guide for Zoning Policy with Emphasis on the Southeast Area,* Denver, Co: The Office, 1961.

Denver (City and County of), Office of Policy Analysis. *Rental Housing Investments in the Inner-City. Neighborhood Stability Research Project* (Research Report H-3), Denver, Co: The Office, 1977.

District of Columbia, Committee on Housing and Urban Development. *Rental Accommodations Act of 1975 (Council Act No. 1-46) and Report... as Referred to the Committee on the District of Columbia, House of Representatives, 94th Congress, 1st session.* Washington, D.C.: U.S. Government Printing Office, 1975.

Drury, Margaret; Olson, Lee; Springer, Michael; and Yap, Lorene. *Lower Income Housing Assistance Program (Section 8): Nationwide Evaluation of the Existing Housing Program.* Washington, D.C.: U.S. Dept. of Housing and Urban Development, 1978.

Durst, Seymour B. "If the Cities Go Down, So Goes the Nation. Urban Analysis and a Prescription for Housing Revival." *Journal of the Institute for Socioeconomic Studies,* Autumn 1977, pp. 25-32.

Eggers, Frederick J. *Background Information and Initial Findings of the Housing Market Practices Survey.* Washington, D.C.: National Committee Against Discrimination in Housing, Inc., 1978.

Ellickson, Phyllis L., and Kanouse, David E. *Codebook for the Attitude Model of the Landlord Survey, Site II, Baseline. Housing Assistance Supply Experiment.* Santa Monica, Calif.: Rand Corp., 1978.

Evans, D. "The Rent Act 1974." *Journal of Planning and Environmental Law,* October 1974, pp. 576-87.

Fairfax County Planning Division. *Student Contribution from Apartments and Mobile Homes.* Fairfax, Vir. 1966.

Falche, Caj O. *Study of Bart's Effects on Property Prices and Rents.* Springfield, Vir.: NTIS, 1978.

Falls Church Planning Office Apartments. *Analysis of Multiple Family Dwelling, The Prospects and Recommendations.* Falls Church, Vir.: 1962.

Fitzgerald, Robert J. "Public Housing Management Budgets: The Performance Funding System." *Journal of Property Management,* May/June 1978, pp. 161-62.

Follain, James R. *Place to Place Indexes of the Price of Housing: Some New Estimates and a Comparative Analysis.* Washington, D.C.: The Urban Institute, 1979.

Follain, James R., and Malpezzi, Stephen. *Dissecting Housing Value and Rent: Estimates of Hedonic Indexes for Thirty-nine Large Standard Metropolitan Statistical Areas.* Washington, D.C.: U.S. Department of Housing and Urban Development, 1979.

Follain, James R., and Malpezzi, Stephen. *Hedonic Indexes for Housing Value and Rent in Thirty-nine Standard Metropolitan Statistical Areas.* Washington, D.C.: U.S. Department of Housing and Urban Development, 1979.

Fougner, Robert S. "33 Long Years of Rent Control." *Real Estate Forum,* 10 January 1977.

Francescato, Guido, et al. "Predicators of Residents' Satisfaction in High Rise and Low Rise Housing." *Journal of Architectural Research,* December 1975, pp. 4-9.

Fredland, J.E., and MacRae, C.D. "FHA Multifamily Financial Failure: A Review of Empirical Studies." *Journal of the American Real Estate & Urban Economics Association,* Spring 1979, pp. 95-122.

Gans, Herbert J. *The Urban Villagers.* New York, N.Y.: Free Press, 1962.

Gillingham, Robert F. *Place-to-place Rent Comparisons Using Hedonic Quality Adjustment Techniques.* Washington, D.C.: U.S. Bureau of Labor Statistics, 1975.

Goodwin, Susan Ann. "Measuring the Value of Housing Quality: A Note." *Journal of Regional Science,* April 1977, pp. 107-15.

Greensboro Planning Department. *Apartment Resident Survey.* Greensboro, N.C.: The Department, 1970.

Greenston, Peter, et al. *Experience in the Section 8 Existing Housing Programs. 1975-76. Part I: Core Analysis.* Washington, D.C.: The Urban Institute, 1977.

Grossman, Howard J. "Apartments in Community Planning: A Suburban Area Case Study." *Urban Land,* January 1966.

Gruen, Gruen & Associates. *Rent Control in New Jersey: The Beginnings.* San Francisco, Calif.: The Associates, 1977.

Haider, Donald H. *The Economics of Condominium Development.* Evanston, Ill: Northwestern University, Center for Urgan Affairs, 1979.

Hakken, Jon. *Discrimination Against Chicanos in the Dallas Rental Housing Market: An Experimental Extension of the Housing Market Practices Survey.* Washington, D.C.: U.S. Department of Housing and Urban Development, 1979.

Halperin, Jerome Y., and Brenner, Michael J. "Opportunities Under the New Section 8 Housing Program." *Real Estate Review,* Spring 1976, pp. 67-75.

Hands, John. "Cooperative Housing Agency: 18 Months On." *Housing Review,* November-December 1978, pp. 148-50.

Harvard-MIT, Joint Center for Urban Studies. *Analysis of Selected Census and Welfare Data to Determine Relation of Household Characteristics, Housing Market Characteristics, and Administrative Welfare Policies to a Direct Housing Assistance Program.* Springfield, Vir.: NTIS, 1974.

Hemel, Eric I. "What Does Rent Control Control? The Urban Poor Increasingly are the Losers in the Rent Controls Game." *Taxing and Spending,* no. 4, 1979, pp. 83-87.

Henderson, J. "Rents, Subsidies for AFDC Recipients Administered by States,

Governed by Federal Policy." *Journal of Housing,* October 1978, pp. 469-70.

Higbee, Edward. *The Squeeze: Cities Without Space.* New York, N.Y.: William Morrow and Company, 1960, pp. 89-138.

Hirsch, Werner Z., and Law, C.K. "Habitability Laws and the Shrinkage of Substandard Rental Housing Stocks." *Urban Studies,* February 1979, pp. 19-28.

Hirsch, Werner Z. and Margolis, Stephen. "Habilitability Laws and Low-Cost Rental Housing." In *Residential Location and Urban Housing Markets.* Edited by Gregory K. Ingram, pp. 181-213. *Studies in Income and Wealth,* vol. 43. Cambridge, Mass.: Ballinger Publishing Company, 1977.

Holley, Paul. *School of Enrollment by Housing Type.* Chicago, Ill.: American Society of Planning Officials, (Planning Advisory Service Report,No. 210.), 1966.

Jackson, Anthony. *A Place Called Home: A History of Low-Cost Housing in Manhattan.* Cambridge, Mass.: MIT Press, 1976.

James, Franklin J., and Lett, Monica R. *The Economics of Rental Housing in New York City: The Effects of Rent Stabilization.* (Prepared for the Rent Stabilization Association of New York City). New York, 1976.

James, Sarah, and Greenston, Peter. *Adoption of an Innovation: Local Housing Authority Participation in Section 8.* Washington, D.C.: The Urban Institute, 1977.

Kaplan, Ethan Z. *Multifamily Housing in St. Louis County: A Survey and Evaluation Report.* Clayton, Missouri: St. Louis County Planning Commission, 1965.

Keller, Suzanne. "Friends and Neighbors in a Planned Community." *Frontiers of Planned Unit Development: A Synthesis of Expert Opinion.* Edited by Robert W. Burchell. New Brunswick, N.J.: Center for Urban Policy Research, 1973, pp. 228-40.

Kochanowski, Paul. "The Rent Control Choice: Some Empirical Findings." *Policy Analysis,* Spring 1980, pp. 171-73+. Empirical analysis of city-enacted rent control ordinances. Forty cities were tested in Connecticut, Massachusetts, and New Jersey.

Kraft, J., and Kraft, A. "Benefits and Costs of Low Rent Public Housing." *Journal of Regional Science,* August 1979, pp. 309-17.

Kriegsfeld, Irving M. "Rent Control: A Plague on Property." *Journal of Property Management,* September/October 1977, pp. 229-33.

Kristof, Frank S. "Housing and People in New York City: A View of the Past, Present and Future." *City Almanac.* February 1976, whole issue.

Kristof, Frank S. "Rent Control Within the Rental Housing Parameters of 1975." *American Real Estate and Urban Economics Association Journal,* Winter 1975, pp. 47-60.

Kuehn, Robert H., et al. *Research and Evaluation Regarding the Section 8 Housing Assistance Program in Sector B: Fair Market Rents for the Existing Housing Program.* Springfield, Vir.: NTIS, 1977.

Lackman, Conway L. "The Classical Base of Modern Rent Theory." *American Journal of Economics and Sociology,* July 1976, pp. 287-300.

Lane, Terry S. *What Families Spend for Housing. The Origins and Uses of the Rules of Thumb.* Springfield, Vir.: NTIS, 1977.

Lange, Irene. *Predicted for Amenities in Apartment Units: A Cross-Sectional Analytic Study.* Sacramento, Calif.: Division of Real Estate, January 1969.

Leepson, Marc. *Rental Housing Shortage.* Washington, D.C.: Washington Editorial Research Reports, 1979, pp. 923-40. (Editorial research reports, 1979, vol. 2, No. 23).

Lett, Monica R. Rent Control: "The Potential for Equity." *American Real Estate and Urban Economics Association Journal,* Spring 1976.

MacNeil, Robert. *The Rental Crunch.* New York, N.Y.: WNET/Thirteen, 1979, p. 9.

Maryland-National Capital Park and Planning Commission. *Dwelling Unit Density, Population, and Potential Public School Enrollment Yield by Existing Zoning Classification for Montgomery and Prince Georges Counties.* Silver Spring, Maryland: The Commission, 1965.

Maryland Department of Housing and Community Development. *Condominiums: Baltimore City.* Baltimore, Maryland: The Department, 1980.

Matthews, John P., and Pappas, James L. "Rent Control and Community Impacts." *Journal of Property Management,* September/October 1979, pp. 265-70.

Mayer, Neil S. *Roles of Lending, Race, Ownership and Neighborhood Changes in Rental Housing Rehabilitation.* Washington, D.C.: U.S. Department of Housing and Urban Development, 1979.

Mayo, Stephen. *Housing Expenditures and Quality. Part I. Report on Housing Expenditures Under a Percent of Rental Housing Allowance. Housing Allowance Demand.* Springfield, Vir.: NTIS, 1977.

Meyerson, Martin; Terrett, Barbara; and Wheaton, William, L.C. *Housing People, and Cities.* New York, N.Y.: McGraw-Hill, 1962.

Mid Willamette Valley Council of Governments. *Neglected Housing Needs: A Low Income Regional Housing Analysis and Data Inventory.* Springfield, Vir.: NTIS, 1973.

Minneapolis Community Planning and Management Team. *Handbook of Tenants' and Landlords' Rights and Duties.* Springfield, Vir.: NTIS, 1973.

Monmouth County Planning Board. *Multi-Family Housing in Monmouth County.* Freehold, N.J.: The Board, 1973.

Moore, Kathi J. "HUD Preemption of Local Rent Control Ordinances—Tenants Entitled to Due Process Rights." *Rutgers Law Review,* Summer 1977, pp. 1025-55.

"Multi-Family Opportunities." *Professional Builder,* September 1979, pp. 114-35.

Nassau County Planning Commission. *Apartments: Their Post and Future Impact on Suburban Living Patterns.* Mineola, N.Y.: The Commission, 1963.

National Association of Realtors, Department of Economics and Research. *Rent Control: A Non-Solution.* Chicago, Ill.: The Association, 1977.

Netuze, Max. *The Suburban Apartment Boom: Case Study of a Land Use Problem.* Baltimore, Maryland: Johns Hopkins University Press, 1968.

New York (City). Temporary Commission on City Finances. *The Effects of Rental Control and Rent Stabilization in New York City;* Fifteenth interim report to the Mayor, New York, N.Y.: The Commission, 1972.

New York Rent Stabilization Law of 1969, The. *"Columbia Law Review,* January 1970, pp. 156-77.

Norcross, Carl, and Hysom, John. *Apartment Communities: The Next Big Market—Who Rents and Why.* Washington, D.C.: Urban Land Institute (ULI Technical Bulletin #61), 1968.

Olmo, Ralph J. "The Paradox of Inflation and Rents." *Journal of Property Management,* January/February 1980, pp. 31-32.

Olsen, Edder O. "An Econometric Analysis of Rent Control." *Journal of Political Economy,* November-December 1972, pp. 1081-100.

O'Toole, Denis. "Sec. 223(f) Rental Housing Program Spurs Resurgence of Activity in HUD/FHA Business." *NAHB Journal-Scope,* 5 May 1975, p. 9.

Ozanne, Larry, and Vanshi, Jean E. *Rehabilitating Central City Housing: Simulations with the Urban Institute Housing Model.* Springfield, Vir.: NTIS, 1978.

Parkins, John A., Jr. "Judicial Attitudes Toward Multiple-Family Dwellings: A Reappraisal." *Washington and Lee Law Review,* Spring 1971, pp. 220-30.

Passaic Valley Citizens Planning Association. *Garden Apartment Study.* Bloomingdale, N.J.: Bloomingdale Planning Board, 1963.

Patrick, Kathryn Lori. "Rent Control: A Practical Guide for Tenant Organizations." *San Diego Law Review* 15 (August 1978): 1185-209.

Peck, James M. "The Case for Ending Rent Control." *New York Law Journal,* 14 April 1976.

Potomac Institute, Washington, D.C. *Rent Control in North America and Four European Countries.* Washington, D.C.: Council for International Urban Liaison, 1977.

Rand Corporation. *Annual Report of the Housing Assistance Supply Experiment.* Santa Monica, Calif.: Rand Corporation, (annual).

Rand Corporation. *Housing Assistance Supply Experiment: Executive Summary.* Springfield, Vir.: NTIS, 1978.

Rasch, Joseph. *New York Rent Control: With All Amendments Through and Including September 1, 1971.* Rochester, N.Y.: Lawyers Co-operative Pub. Co., 1971.

Raymond, Parish, Pine and Weiner, Inc. *Condominiums in the District of Columbia: The Impact of Conversions of Washington's Citizens, Neighborhoods and Housing Stock.* Washington, D.C.: U.S. Department of Housing and Urban Development, 1975.

"Rent Control: Nobody Wins, Everybody Loses." *Realtors Review,* February 1977.

"Rent Control Update." *Housing Law Bulletin,* July/August 1979, pp. 9-11.

"Rezoning Suburbia." *Progressive Architecture,* May 1971, pp. 92-94.

Rhode Island Department of Community Affairs. *The Rhode Island Apartment Occupant: An Analysis and Review.* July 1972.

Rhyne, Charles S. et al. *Municipalities and Multiple Residential Housing: Condominiums and Rent Control.* Washington, D.C.: National Institute of Municipal Law Officers, 1975.

Richardson, Harry W. "On the Possibility of Positive Rent Gradients." *Journal of Urban Economics,* January 1977, pp. 60-68.

Rolde, (L. Robert) Company. *Garden Apartments and School-Age Children.* Washington, D.C.: National Association of Home Builders, 1962.

Rosen, K.T. "A Regional Model of Multifamily Housing Starts." *Journal of the American Real Estate & Urban Economics Association,* Spring 1979, pp. 63-76.

Rosenthal, Jack. "The Suburban Apartment Boom," In *Suburbia in Transition.* Edited by Louis H. Masotti and Jeffrey K. Hadden. New York: New Viewpoints, 1974, pp. 28-31.

Rydell, C. Peter. *Effects of Market Conditions on Prices and Profits of Rental Housing.* Santa Monica, Calif. Rand Corporation, September 1977.

Rydell, C. Peter. *Rental Housing in Site I: Characteristics of the Capital Stock at Baseline.* Santa Monica, Calif. Rand Corp., 1975.

Rydell, C. Peter, and Friedman, Joseph. *Rental Housing on Site I. Market Structure and Conditions at Baseline. Supply Experiment of the Experimental Housing Allowance Program.* Springfield, Vir.: NTIS, 1975.

Salamon, Lester M. *The Substandard Rental Housing in Durham: Toward an Inner-City Housing Policy.* Durham, N.C.: Durham Urban Observatory, 1976.

Sather, Kent N. "Analyzing Apartment Market Characteristics." *Journal of Property Management,* September/October 1970, pp. 231-33.

Schafer, Robert. *Maintenance and Operating Behavior of Resident and Absentee Landlords.* Cambridge, Mass.: Harvard University, Dept. of City and Regional Planning, 1977.

Schafer, Robert. *The Suburbanization of Multifamily Housing,* Lexington, Mass.: Lexington Books, 1974.

Schare, Ann Burnet. *Externalties, Segregation, and Housing Prices.* Washington, D.C.: The Urban Institute, 1975.

Schwartz, Jeffrey B. "Phase II Rent Stabilization." *Urban Lawyer,* Summer 1972, pp. 417-32.

Shanley, Michael G., and Hotchkiss, Charles M. *How Low-Income Renters Buy Homes. Housing Assistance Supply Experiment.* Springfield, Vir.: NTIS, 1979.

Shreiber, Chanoch, and Tabriztchi, Sirousse. "Rent Control in New York City:

A Proposal to Improve Resource Allocation." *Urban Affairs Quarterly.* June 1976, pp. 511-22.

Silver, Jennifer, and Shreve, Cathy. *Condominium Conversion Controls: An Information Bulletin of the Community and Economic Development Task Force of the Urban Consortium.* Washington, D.C.: U.S. Department of Housing and Urban Development, 1979.

South Florida Regional Planning Council. *Housing: The Regional View.* Miami, Fla.: The Council, 1975.

Southern California Association of Governments. *Housing Locator, Section 8: Rental Assistance Opportunities. A Guide to Assisted Rental Housing in Los Angeles, Ventura, Orange, Riverside, San Bernadino, and Imperial Counties.* Washington, D.C.: U.S. Department of Housing and Urban Development, 1980.

Stanfield, Rochelle L. "Caught in the Squeeze of the Rental Housing Market." *National Journal,* 17 February 1979, pp. 262-65.

Stanton, Richard E., and Britt, Therman, P. *Audit of Baseline Landlord Survey in Site I. Housing Assistance Supply Experiment.* Santa Monica, Calif.: Rand Corp., 1977.

Starr, Roger. "An End to Rental Housing." *Public Interest,* Fall, 1979, pp. 25-38.

Stegman, Michael A. "Multifamily Distress: A Case for National Action." *Journal of the American Real Estate & Urban Economics Association,* Spring 1979, pp. 77-94.

Stegman, Michael A. *Nonmetropolitan Urban Housing: An Economic Analysis of Problems and Policies.* Cambridge, Mass.: Ballinger Pub. Co., 1976.

Stegman, Michael A. "Trouble for Multifamily Housing: Its Effects on Conserving Older Neighborhoods." *Occasional Papers in Housing and Community Affairs* 2 (1979): pp. 233-37.

Stegman, Michael A., and Sumka, Howard J. *The Dynamics of Nonmetropolitan Urban Rental Housing Markets: A comparative Analysis.* Springfield, Vir.: NTIS, 1976.

Stegman, Michael A., and Sumka, Howard J. "Income Elasticities of Demand For Rental Housing in Small Cities." *Urban Studies,* February 1978, pp. 51-61.

Stegman, Michael A., and Sumka, Howard J. "Nonmetropolitan and Inner-City Housing Investment Markets." *American Real Estate and Urban Economics Association Journal,* Fall, 1974, pp. 81-99.

Sternlieb, George. *The Garden Apartment Development: A Municipal Cost-Revenue Analysis.* New Brunswick, N.J.: Bureau of Economic Research, Rutgers University, 1964.

Sternlieb, George, et al. *A Study of Rent Control in the Greater Miami Beach Luxury Housing Market.* New Brunswick, N.J.: Center for Urban Policy Research, Rutgers University, 1977.

Sternlieb, George, and Brody, Elizabeth. "The Pitfalls in Rent Control." *Real Estate Review,* Summer 1974, pp. 120-24.

Sternlieb, G., and Burchell, R.W. "Multifamily Housing Demand: 1980-2000." *Journal of American Real Estate and Urban Economics Association*, Spring 1979, pp. 1-38.

Sternlieb, George, and Hughes, James W., "Rent Control's Impact on the Community Tax Base." *Appraisal Journal*, July 1979, pp. 381-94.

Striech, Patricia, et al. *Multifamily Federal Rental Housing Assistance Programs in Canada and the United States: A Comparative Study*. Springfield, Vir.: NTIS, 1980.

Stucker, James P. *Rent Inflation in Brown County, Wisconsin: 1973-1978. Housing Assistance Supply Experiment*. Santa Monica, Calif.: Rand Corporation, 1978.

Stull, William J. "The Landlord's Dilemma: Asking Rent Strategies in a Heterogeneous Housing Market." *Journal of Urban Economics*, January 1978, pp. 101-15.

Sussna, Stephen. "What the Courts Say About Anti-Apartment Zoning." *Buildings*, March 1972, pp. 64-65.

Syracuse, Lee A. *Arguments for Apartment Zoning*. Washington, D.C.: National Association of Home Builders, 1968.

Temple University-Center for Social Policy and Community Development. *Leasing Procedures for Housing Managers: Instructor's Guide*. Washington, D.C.: U.S. Department of Housing and Urban Development, 1979.

Temple University-Center for Social Policy and Community Development. *Leasing Procedures for Housing Managers: Participant's Workbook*. Washington, D.C.: U.S. Department of Housing and Urban Development, 1979.

Temple University-Center for Social Policy and Community Development. *Litigation Regulations and Guidelines in Housing Management: Instructor's Manual*. Washington, D.C.: U.S. Department of Housing and Urban Development, 1979.

Temple University-Center for Social Policy and Community Development. *Litigation Regulations and Guidelines in Housing Management. Participants Workbook*. Washington, D.C.: U.S. Department of Housing and Urban Development, 1979.

Teplin, Albert M. *The Scope of Residential Rent Control Laws: A Preliminary Study*. Washington, D.C.: U.S. Board of Governors of the Federal Reserve System, 1977.

Touche, Ross and Company. *The Impact and Effects of Section 167(k) on the Rehabilitation of Multifamily Property. Volume I*. Springfield, Vir.: NTIS, 1974.

Touche, Ross and Company. *Operations Review of the South Bend Housing Allowance Office. Implications for On-Going Programs*. Springfield, Vir.: NTIS, 1977.

Touche, Ross and Company. *Study on Tax Considerations in Multifamily Housing Investments*. Springfield, Vir.: NTIS, 1971.

Touche, Ross and Company. *Study on Tax Considerations in Multifamily Housing Investments: 1967-1977, Vol. 1: Parts I-X*. Springfield, Vir.: NTIS, 1977.

Touche, Ross and Company. *Study on Tax Considerations in Multifamily Housing Investments: 1976-1977, Vol. 2. Appendices.* Springfield, Vir.: NTIS, 1977.

Trolley, George S., and Diamond, Douglas B. *Homeownership, Rental Housing and Tax Incentives.* Springfield, Vir.: NTIS, 1977.

Trowbridge, Carl R. "The relation of gross multipliers to interest rates." *Real Estate Appraiser,* July-August, 1976, pp. 20-24.

Ungar, Diane. "Emergency Tenant Protection in New York: Ten Years of Rent Stabilization." *Fordham Urban Law Journal* 7, no. 2 (1978-79): 305-35.

U.S. Bureau of the Census. *Current Housing Reports: Characteristics of Apartments Completed: 1975.* Washington, D.C.: The Bureau (Quarterly).

U.S. Bureau of the Census. *Current Housing Reports: Housing Vacancies. Vacancy Rates and Characteristics of Housing in the United States: Annual Statistics, 1974.* Washington, D.C.: The Bureau.

U.S. Bureau of the Census. *Current Housing Reports: Housing Vacancies. Vacancy Rates and Characteristics of Housing in the United States: Annual Statistics, 1976.* Washington, D.C.: The Bureau (annual).

U.S. Bureau of the Census. *Current Housing Reports: Market Absorption of Apartments: Annual, 1975.* Washington, D.C.: The Bureau (annual).

U.S. Bureau of the Census and U.S. Department of Housing and Urban Development. *Annual Housing Survey 1973.* Washington, D.C.: The Department (annual).

U.S. Bureau of Economic Analysis, Regional Economic Measurement Division. *Local Area Personal Income 1971-1976* (all sections). Washington, D.C.: The Bureau, 1978.

U.S. Congress. House. Committee on the District of Columbia. *Authorizing the District of Columbia Council to Regulate and Stabilize Rents in the District of Columbia: Report Together with Minority Views to Accompany H.R. 4771.* Washington, D.C.: U.S. Government Printing Office, 1973. (93rd Congress, 1st session. House. Report No. 93-259).

U.S. Congress. House. Committee on the District of Columbia. Subcommittee on Commerce, Housing and Transportation. *Rental Accommodations Act of 1975 (Council Act No. 1-46). Hearing and Disposition, 94th Congress, 1st session on H. Con. Res. 399, October 1 and 6, 1975.* Washington, D.C.: U.S. Government Printing Office, 1979.

U.S. Congress. House. Committee on Government Operations. Manpower and Housing Subcommittee. *Preemption of Local Rent Control Laws by HUD. Hearing, 95th Congress, 1st session, December 2, 1977.* Washington: U.S. Government Printing Office, 1979.

U.S. Congress, Senate Committee on Banking. Housing and Urban Affairs. *Condominium Housing Issues,* 96th Congress, 1st session, 28 June 1979.

U.S. Congress. Senate. Committee on the District of Columbia. *Fiscal Pressures on the District of Columbia. Hearing, 94th Congress, 2d session, March 30, 1976.* Washington, D.C.: U.S. Government Printing Office, 1976.

U.S. Congress. Senate. Committee on the District of Columbia. Subcommittee on Public Health, Education, Welfare, and Safety. *Rent Control Act of 1973. Hearings, 93d Congress, 1st session, on H.R. 4771, July 24, 1973.* Washington, D.C.: U.S. Government Printing Office, 1973.

U.S. Department of Housing and Urban Development. *The Conversion of Rental Housing to Condominiums and Cooperatives: A National Study of Scope, Causes and Impacts (+Appendices).* Washington, D.C.: U.S. GPO, 1980.

U.S. Department of Housing and Urban Development. *Economic Analysis of the Proposed Rental Housing Programs.* Washington, D.C.: The Department, 1973.

U.S. Department of Housing and Urban Development. *The Experimental Housing Allowance Program.* Washington, D.C.: The Department, 1974.

U.S. Department of Housing and Urban Development. *Lower Income Housing Assistance Program (Section 8)–Nationwide Evaluation of the Existing Housing Program.* Washington, D.C.: The Department, 1979.

U.S. Department of Housing and Urban Development. *Problems Affecting Federally-Supported Low Rent Public Housing.* Washington, D.C.: The Department, 1979.

U.S. Department of Housing and Urban Development. *Research Design of Rental Conversions to Condominiums and Cooperatives.* Washington, D.C.: The Department, 1979.

U.S. Department of Housing and Urban Development. *Research Design of Rental Conversions to Condominiums and Cooperatives.* Washington, D.C.: The Department, 1979.

U.S. Department of Housing and Urban Development. *Section 8 Housing Assistance Payments Program: Existing Housing: A Policy Paper.* Washington, D.C.: The Department, 1976.

U.S. Department of Housing and Urban Development. *Section 8 Housing Assistance Payments Program: The Loan Management Set Aside. A Field Study.* Washington, D.C.: The Department, 1977.

U.S. Department of Housing and Urban Development. *Special Rental Subsidy Analysis.* Washington, D.C.: The Department, 1973.

U.S. Federal Energy Administration. *Analysis of a Retrofit for Low-Income Consumers.* Springfield, Vir.: NTIS, 1974.

U.S. General Accounting Office. *District of Columbia's Rent Establishment Policies and Procedures Need Improvement: Report to the Congress.* Washington, D.C.: The Office, 1978.

U.S. General Accounting Office. *Rental Housing: A National Problem that Needs Immediate Attention.* Washington, D.C.: U.S. GPO, 1979.

U.S. General Accounting Office. *Section 236 Rental Housing: An Assessment of HUD's Comments on GAO's Evaluations.* Washington, D.C.: The Office, 1978.

Urban Systems Research and Engineering. *Report on Housing Quality Standards in the Section 8 Existing Housing Program.* Springfield, Vir.: NTIS, (n.d.).

Urban Systems Research and Engineering. *Report on the Section 8 New Construction Program.* Springfield, Vir.: NTIS (n.d.).

Urban Systems Research and Engineering, Inc. *Research and Evaluation Regarding the Section 8 Housing Assistance Program. Report on Section 8 Existing Fair Market Rents.* Springfield, Vir.: NTIS, 1977.

Utt, Ronald, D. "Rent Control: History's Unlearned Lesson." *Real Estate Review.* Spring 1978, pp. 87-90.

Utt, Ronald D. *Rent Control-Sixty Years of Unlearned Lessons.* New York: National Association of Real Estate Investment Trusts, May/June 1977.

Virginia. Housing Development Authority. *Section 8 Housing Assistance Payments Program: Existing Housing Procedural Manual.* Richmond, Vir., 1975, p. 69.

Walker & Dunlop. *"Rent Control: Are the Benefits Worth the Costs?"* Portfolio, Washington, Spring 1976.

Walsh, J.A. "An Analysis of Intraurban Residential Ownership Patterns." *Environment and Planning,* 10 January 1978, pp. 17-20.

Weaver, Robert C. "Rental Housing: An Endangered Species?" *Journal of Property Management,* September/October 1979, pp. 271-74.

Weaver, Robert C. "Rental Housing: An Endangered Species?" *Mortgage Banker,* February 1979, pp. 52-56.

Westat, Inc. *Section 8 Research Program Housing Quality Standards and Inspection.* Springfield, Vir.: NTIS, (n.d.).

Westat, Inc. *Section 8 Research Program New Construction.* Springfield, Vir.: NTIS (n.d.).

Westat, Inc. *Section 8 Research Program PHA Administrative Functions and Fees.* Springfield, Vir.: NTIS, (n.d.).

Westat, Inc. *Section 8 Research Program Participating and Non-Participating Landlords.* Springfield, Vir.: NTIS, (n.d.).

Westat, Inc. *Section 8 Research Program PHA and Jurisdictional Participation.* Springfield, Vir.: NTIS, (n.d.).

Westat, Inc. *Section 8 Research Program Recipients and Non-Recipients.* Springfield, Vir.: NTIS, (n.d.).

Westat, Inc. *Section 8 Research Program Summary Report.* Springfield, Vir.: NTIS, (n.d.).

Westchester County Department of Planning. *Residential Analysis for West Chester County, New York. Factors Affecting the Cost of Used Housing.* Springfield, Vir.: NTIS, 1974.

Wetherington, Wade. "The District of Columbia Rental Housing Act of 1977: The Effect of Rent Control on the Rental Housing Market." *Catholic University Law Review;* Spring 1978, pp. 607-26.

White, Michelle J. "On the Short-term Effects of Long-term Change in Cities: An Efficient Land Market Model." *Journal of Urban Economics,* October 1978, pp. 485-504.

White, Sammis B. *Market Intermediaries and Indirect Suppliers: First Year Report for Site 11. Supply Experiment of the Experimental Housing Allowance Program.* Santa Monica, Calif.: Rand Corp., 1977.

"Why do People Rent. . . and Who are They?" *Realtors Review.* April 1978, pp. 9-11+.

Yap, Lorene; Greenston, Peter; and Sadacca, Robert. *Lower Income Housing Assistance Program (Section 8): Nationwide Evaluation of the Existing Housing Program: Technical Supplement.* Washington, D.C.: U.S. Department of Housing and Urban Development, 1978.

Index

Abandonment, 49, 110

Affluent, decline of interest in rental facilities, 3, 97

AHS. *See* Annual Housing Survey

Annual Housing Survey (AHS), 6, 36, 45

Black central city renter households, 4-5, 23-26; income, 29-31, 66

Central cities, 112, 114-15

Condominiums and co-ops, conversion from rental housing, 94-95, 97-98, 122-31; displacement of former tenants, 127-28; government regulation, 130-31; household composition, 125-27; impact on community, 128-29; in metropolitan areas, 123-24; post conversion residents, 129-30

Costs of rental housing, 12. *See also* Financial costs; Operating costs

CPS. *See* Current Population Survey

Current Population Survey (CPS), 6-7, 36, 45-46

Deletion of supply, 49, 54-55, 103-08; age of structures, 106-09; and household composition, 108-09; effect of rent levels, 111-12; in urban areas, 112, 114-15; national overview, 103-04; regional variations, 104, 106; size of structures, 106. *See also* Condominiums and co-ops, conversions from rental housing; Supply

Demand: forecasting, 6-7, 14-15, 41-44, 100; household configuration, effect on, 3-7, 37-38, 41-42

Demand versus supply, 9-11, 95-97

Demographic changes, 17, 19, 57

Detroit, 112, 114

Facilities, 55

Female headed households, 24-26, 29, 45

Financing costs of rental housing, 87-91; mortgages, 86, 96; rent increases, 87-88

Government subsidies, 92-93

Homeownership, 11-12, 76-82; as protection against inflation, 96; household configurations, 3-4, 37-38; income-house value ratios, 11, 78-81; mortgages, 79-80, 96

Homeowner versus renter status. *See* Renter versus owner status

Household configurations, 3-7, 13, 39-40, 108-09; changes in, 17-19, 40-41; one-person households, 19; renter/owner comparisons, 3-5, 20-23; size of 55, 71-73. *See also* Black central city households; Female headed households; Homeownership, household configurations; Renter households; Two-income households

Income, 5, 9-10, 15, 65-66, 100-01, 110

Industrialization, effect on housing, 13, 15, 92